Entreprene
To **Investor**
The **Hard Way**

Entrepreneur To Investor The Hard Way

David L. Durgin

with

Sherry Robinson

SANTA FE

Sunstone books may be purchased for educational, business, or sales promotional
use. For information please write: Special Markets Department, Sunstone Press,
P.O. Box 2321, Santa Fe, New Mexico 87504-2321.

Cover photograph by Douglas Merriam

Book design › Vicki Ahl
Body typeface › ITC New Baskerville ❖ Display typeface › Broadway
Printed on acid free paper

Library of Congress Cataloging-in-Publication Data

Durgin, David L., 1938-
  Entrepreneur to investor the hard way / by David L. Durgin, with Sherry Robin-
son.
      p. cm.
  Includes index.
  ISBN 978-0-86534-695-6 (softcover : alk. paper)
  1. Entrepreneurship–New Mexico. 2. Technology transfer–Economic aspects–New
Mexico. 3. Venture capital–New Mexico. 4. New business enterprises–New Mexico.
5. Businessmen–New Mexico–Albuquerque–Biography. 6. Capitalists and financiers-
-New Mexico–Albuquerque–Biography. 7. Durgin, David L., 1938- I. Robinson,
Sherry. II. Title.
  HB615.D874 2008
  338.9789092–dc22
  [B]
                          2008033389

WWW.SUNSTONEPRESS.COM
SUNSTONE PRESS / POST OFFICE BOX 2321 / SANTA FE, NM 87504-2321 /USA
(505) 988-4418 / ORDERS ONLY (800) 243-5644 / FAX (505) 988-1025

Dedicated
To
My Family

Contents

Introduction

In the future people will have ten careers (not ten jobs) during their lives, say workforce prognosticators. David L. Durgin has nearly reached that number.

During a long engineering and bootstrapped business and investment career, Dave has worn the mantles of Cold Warrior, Sandian, Defense Contractor, Tech-Transfer Consultant, High-Tech Entrepreneur, Manufacturer, Angel Investor, Mentor, and Venture Capitalist. The role he probably relished the most was Mentor.

Dave's professional journey parallels Albuquerque, New Mexico's evolution from a government town to a birthplace of technology transfer to a modern city with a diversified economy that includes a vibrant technology sector. Through it all, Dave posted a number of firsts.

One enterprise at a time, he helped transform the city's economy. Today Albuquerque has 21 companies that bear his fingerprints and his investments. He also worked in various initiatives and groups to improve the business climate in Albuquerque and New Mexico.

"He's a guy who is internally driven to make things better," said entrepreneur Lem Hunter. "Some people want to be a hero and dash in when there's a fire. Some are just there when times are good. Dave just wants things to be better. He's not in this just for the money."

Dave wasn't all business. Another role was husband and parent to seven children—three daughters (two adopted, one biological) of his own, two stepchildren of his wife Eilene, and two step granddaughters (Dave and Eilene are legal guardians). His family wasn't sheltered from the whiplash of Dave's business ups and downs, nor was it immune to the complexities of a blended family or the fallout of modern life. Dave cares deeply about his wife and family members, but out of respect for their privacy, has limited his discussion of their lives.

Dave could have followed his father and brother into the CIA—and did, briefly—but from his teens, electronics held his quick, if rebellious, mind, and he pursued the field through technician training to be recruited by Sandia Laboratory in 1961. The Cold War was accelerating, which created new demands on the lab, and Dave arrived as Sandia was modernizing its nuclear stockpile.

He got useful exposure to manufacturing, and he was involved in atmospheric nuclear testing in the South Pacific when the team discovered that a nuclear effect called Electromagnetic Pulse, or EMP, could harm electrical and electronic systems. It was both threat and opportunity. His work in EMP would later take him into some high-powered management positions with defense contractors.

In 1967, Dave became one of the first to leave Sandia and attempt technology transfer. A family man with two children, he said goodbye to a secure job and paycheck and started a business to commercialize technology. Business and lab vocabularies didn't yet include the words "tech transfer" or "high-tech entrepreneur." The business climate in Albuquerque and New Mexico, still heavily dependent on federal spending, was hardly welcoming. And nothing in Dave's training prepared him to run a business. His Product Designs Inc. lasted just over a year, but he made significant progress toward his MBR, Master's in Business Reality.

"Having a failure first is probably better in terms of managing humility," Dave would say later.

After months of anxiety during PDI's decline, Dave landed at BDM, an emerging Albuquerque defense contractor. The Cold War had saved Sandia by providing a new mission after World War II, and it was a boon to companies doing business with the government. From the early 1960s to the end of the Cold War, Albuquerque and the state would see a growing number of government contractors that added thousands of paychecks to the local economy. Dave rose through the ranks to join BDM's management team. In the process he had an inside view of defense agency operations and contractors.

In 1979, recruited to start a nuclear practice, he joined the venerable consulting firm Booz Allen Hamilton. As a partner, he had autonomy and a bigger organizational and financial base to grow a company. He opened an Albuquerque office and eventually became a senior partner.

By the late 1980s, Dave and others privy to government intelligence were starting to ask, "What if we win?"

The federal government was spending upwards of $140 billion a year on research and development, but little of it was commercialized for public use. At the same time, Japan had become a threat to the United States' competitive position. New Mexico was precariously dependent on declining defense spending. It was obvious to Dave and others that if peace broke out, New Mexico could be in real trouble.

The answer to many problems, it seemed, was technology transfer—the passage of technology developed in government and university labs into the public realm as new products. Dave, with his long background in electronics, Sandia and defense contracting, was uniquely qualified to participate and lead this new movement. With his old friend Jim Schwarz, who had a similar career path, and several others, Dave launched Quatro Corporation in 1989. It was the first company formed in New Mexico to commercialize technology.

The reality of tech transfer was quite different from the hype. It was a difficult, expensive, risky process. New Mexico had no technologies on the shelf ready for the magic of development and marketing. Dave and his partners became consultants as they continued the search but quickly realized they needed financing and manufacturing. The state had no venture capitalists and virtually no contract manufacturing, so

Quatro added those capabilities to the company's menu.

In 1989 Quatro began the long process of commercializing its first technology, which would result, several years and many dollars later, in Quasar Inc. Quatro became the poster child of tech transfer and the scene of many a political photo opportunity.

Even so, Dave could see that the business climate in Albuquerque and New Mexico wouldn't support technology transfer and new technology startup companies. His own fund was the only venture-type entity to survive the economic slump of the late 1980s, and New Mexico was still not on the radar of the nation's investors. There were no support organizations. He joined a handful of other visionaries trying to diversify New Mexico's economy and drag the state into the 1990s. In that capacity he either led or participated in a host of initiatives, organizations and task forces.

"Dave is one of the most influential people in the community because so many wires go through him," said his old friend and former business partner Jim Schwarz.

Quatro's diverse activities catapulted it into new arenas and accelerated its growth while ballooning costs and debt, which strained the partnership. After an initially fractious split, Dave negotiated a more agreeable parting. He spun out segments of the business to three partners and took command of the two operations that mattered most to him—tech transfer-investment and manufacturing. Quatro survived.

His trials weren't over. His manufacturing company entered a massive, costly deal with a corporate giant that reneged on its contract. In one of the most trying episodes of his business life, Dave navigated a lopsided, two-year court battle and bankruptcy. He emerged not exactly unscathed but with his investment operation intact and more credits toward his MBR. He learned again that failure, however brutal, isn't fatal.

As his fortunes waned in manufacturing, they waxed as an investor. His first three investments in New Mexico technology companies performed well, setting the stage for Dave's rise as an angel investor. His Quatro Ventures became the pioneer fund in commercializing technology in New Mexico. In the process he honed his model of money and mentoring—intense involvement with portfolio companies, which greatly improves their chances of success, and investments at critical periods.

"Dave invests not just his money but his time," said entrepreneur Rich Hoke. "He invests Dave Durgin in them."

As the deals evolved, so did Dave. He gained a more sophisticated understanding of people, business models, startup financing and the world of venture capitalists. When he became a special limited partner in an out-of-state venture fund, it was a cultural leap to be a venture capitalist. It was a natural trajectory, but he had always identified more with the entrepreneur.

In 2003, Dave took a bigger step with partners Ray Radosevich, former dean of the University of New Mexico business school and a fellow investor, and Tom Stephenson, an Albuquerque native who represented a Texas venture fund. They organized Verge Fund, the first New Mexico-based venture-capital fund with the goal of investing only in New Mexico companies. Verge specialized in early-stage technology companies and seed-capital investments because financing for the newest, smallest startups had always been the most difficult, as Dave and his partners well knew.

"Verge was needed a long time ago," said entrepreneur Ron McPhee, a special limited partner.

Launching Verge required going against what "everybody" said was impossible. Everybody said it was impossible to raise money in New Mexico. Everybody said it was impossible to find worthwhile deals in New Mexico. Everybody said it was impossible to grow and sustain high-tech companies in New Mexico. Everybody was wrong.

In just four years, Verge had a portfolio of 15 successful companies and had been named one of the nation's Top 100 Venture Capital Firms for Entrepreneurs by Entrepreneur Magazine. When the National Venture Capital Association heralded New Mexico as first in growth between 1997 and 2007, it was Dave whom Business Week wanted to interview.

"In Quatro Ventures, Dave was always trying to create the funds that could be invested in seed deals in New Mexico," said entrepreneur Rich Hoke. "Dave's lifelong dream culminated in Verge. It was something he'd been working toward ever since I met him. With Verge, he hit his stride."

1

Coming of Age

David L. Durgin's first experience in business was catching crabs on Chesapeake Bay and selling them door to door for $1.25 a dozen, although customers were sometimes amused to learn that, to this five-year-old, a dozen meant six. Besides the promise of immediate riches, the physical exertion of his soggy enterprise was exhilarating.

He had just spent 18 months in a full-body cast after contracting Perthes Disease, an affliction of young children, usually boys, which causes the hip joint to degenerate. Today it's treated by crutches, casts, traction and physical therapy, but in the early 1940s, doctors weren't sure he'd walk again. For long months, Dave was a small, talking statue, hauled around in a wagon by his parents and brother Lane.

Dave has little memory of this episode, but it probably contributed to his life-long drive to make things happen and to his impatience—core qualities of an entrepreneur. He would never again be a passive observer.

War Years

Dave's father, Henry Lawrence (Larry) Durgin, was born and raised in Lewiston, Maine. At 6 feet 3 inches and 250 pounds, he was a formidable man and a good athlete. After playing football at Dartmouth, Larry worked in the family insurance business and later became a math teacher, sports broadcaster and high school and college football coach.

His mother, Jean Fosdick Durgin, was born in Somerville, Massachusetts. A talented artist and musician who spoke several languages, she had been a concert harpist and hosted a radio cooking show called "Meat on the Table" before meeting Larry. The two were married in 1933. Brother Lane was born in 1935. By the time Dave was born, on June 14, Flag Day, 1938, the threat of conflict loomed over Europe and Asia.

At the beginning of World War II, the Navy wanted a corps of young men who were familiar with the coastline to patrol against German U-boats. Larry completed officer training, but the program was cancelled. Given the choice of being drafted or accepting a Navy commission, he chose the Navy. From 1942 to 1946 he served in the Naval Air Transport Service as a communications officer, traveling to the Middle East and Africa, where he built communications systems to support the troops. The family lived at Opalocka Naval Air Station in Florida and Pautuxent Naval Air Station in Maryland.

The onset of Dave's illness was in Florida. "They thought he might not walk again. It was pretty traumatic," Lane said. "I remember dragging him around in a cart. He was pretty happy, as I remember. We'd take him to the beach and lay him down in the sand." There the two boys saw fragments of American ships torpedoed by German U-boats wash up on the beach where they played. Thanks to Navy doctors, Dave recovered completely but probably would have grown a few inches taller (he's 5'11") without the disease.

Larry was away for long periods of time, so Jean was on her own. "Mom ran the family," recalled Lane. "She did everything." She and the boys had help and support from other Navy families, and those friends would help the Durgins pull through Dave's time in the body cast and their mother's near fatal illness. "Another military couple, Elm and Iola Hintz, stepped in and helped take care of us," Dave said.

As the Durgins moved during the war, the family's social circle changed often, which wasn't unusual for military families. "I met all kinds of people—my father's friends and their wives and kids," Dave said. "My parents were always taking in young sailors and providing them with a home away from home. We formed temporary family structures and then moved on and did it again. It didn't bother me at all. I don't remember issues with meeting people—I just sort of jumped in."

This ease with new people, new situations and change would serve Dave his entire life, personally and in business: "Change is a healthy thing," he said. "My first boss at Sandia Lab retired after 42 years. I can't imagine myself doing anything for 42 years."

Farmer's Son

When Larry Durgin got out of the Navy in 1946, he decided to chase his dream of becoming a gentleman farmer. The Durgins bought a 100-acre farm in Lyme, New Hampshire. The house, built around 1789, was the former Muskrat Inn, located on the banks of the Connecticut River. They renovated the house, lifting the entire inn to build a sprawling basement underneath, and added a 21-ton fireplace that would burn five-foot logs. They also renovated the barn and utility shed.

The family planted acres of vegetables, started nearly 100,000 seedlings in their own greenhouse and raised chickens. The farm had regular summer routes. Jean, driving the truck, sold vegetables, frozen chickens and eggs to grocery stores, summer camps and hotels. "She had a mink coat she'd wear to sell eggs," Lane recalled.

"We spent a good part of the winter getting ready for spring," Dave said. "We started seedlings for spring planting. We spent entire nights, in shifts, literally herding chickens. We had to keep the chickens moving so they didn't freeze to death, and we had to watch for predators." In the basement of the house, they killed and processed chickens. Dave couldn't eat chicken for a long time after that.

Dave entered third grade at Lyme Elementary School, the third school he had attended. The four-room schoolhouse had two grades in each room. He graduated from the eighth grade there. These five years were a period of calm and stability after the war.

When Dave was about 12 or 13, his parents gave up at truck farming.

"When we weren't helping with the farm, there was plenty for boys to do—fishing and canoeing on the river and hunting of all kinds. We weren't enslaved," Dave said. "Winters in New Hampshire were brutal. The temperature could be below zero for weeks on end—

temperatures of 30 or 40 below zero were common—and we were often snowed in. My brother and I shared a room and had a small radio between our beds. We'd lie there at night and listen to baseball—the Boston Braves."

After five years, farming had exhausted the family resources. "I didn't realize until I was in business that cash flow on a farm had to be a nightmare," Dave said. "They decided to leave the farm. If this was a bitter disappointment, my parents didn't let on. They were both New Englanders and incredibly private. My father was very reserved, very quiet. They never talked about it, at least not in front of us."

Period of Insanity

In 1950, through old Navy connections, Larry Durgin became a recruiter for the CIA, then a relatively new agency. (It was authorized by President Truman in 1947.) In 1952 Larry joined the CIA full time in communications operations, and he and Jean moved to Washington, D.C. Dave and Lane stayed in New Hampshire to attend Kimball Union Academy, a respected boys' prep school, on scholarship. On graduation, Lane turned down an opportunity to attend the University of New Hampshire and followed his father into the CIA where he would have a distinguished thirty-year career.

Two of the three Durgin men were now Cold Warriors; Jean and Dave would, in time, join them. To this day, Dave calls the CIA "the family business."

As the Durgins had enjoyed their peaceful country life and the nation recovered from World War II, communism was expanding through Eastern Europe. The Soviet Union, with the help of captured German scientists, developed its own atom bomb, along with an aircraft capable of delivering it. The slumbering Russian bear had become a new threat.

In 1953, Kimball Union's headmaster wrote: "Make no mistake: these are troubled times. But they are also times of rich promise. If we stand on the threshold of an atomic Armageddon, so also do we stand upon the threshold of an atomic Age of Gold." The United States had catapulted the world into the Atomic Age, and everyone—from military brass to high school headmasters—was acutely sensitive to it.

Dave, like most teenagers, was exuberantly unaware of these new tensions. "My freshman year was fairly normal—I was active in sports and earned pretty good grades. I never knew I had leadership skills until I noticed people following me, and it wasn't always to good ends."

His working scholarship included a job in the academy's kitchen, where the head chef befriended him. The summer after his freshman year, the chef offered him a job. Would he be interested in working in the kitchen and serving as a camp councilor at a girls' camp?

"There were 30 female councilors and lots of partying. I fell for a gorgeous, blonde Swede, the archery instructor. I was 15. I traveled to New York to meet her parents, and they wisely made sure it didn't go any farther. I recovered quickly and later that summer I got a job with a traveling circus. I set up tents, worked the concessions and was a bouncer at the girlie show. I got paid a dollar an hour as long as I was awake."

The genie of fun was out of the bottle, and hormones had kicked in. Dave's sophomore year was a wild ride with no seatbelts.

"I would take off with friends and disappear from school to go to Boston or New York." A classmate wrote in Dave's yearbook that year, "I hope you don't take any more night trips to NY. If you do, coach will bounce you for sure this time."

"My grandfather was then commuting between Maine and Boston and had a suite at the Parker House, a hotel he and his buddies owned for a while. I occasionally visited him in Boston."

Jean's stepfather, Dave's grandfather, was George Washington Lane, banker and entrepreneur. "He started working in the bank in Lewiston, Maine as a janitor," said Dave's brother Lane. "By the time he died, he owned the bank. It was the only bank in Maine to remain open through the Depression. He never went to high school."

Said Dave: "He was a real entrepreneur and an early influence on me. We used to talk and play cards. He was always off doing something interesting."

G.W. Lane's other businesses included a part ownership of the exclusive Poland Springs Resort and the Poland Springs Water Company. He was friends with hotelier Howard Johnson, who gave the two Durgin boys each a silver dollar during their visit to his summer home. He was a political mentor of Sen. Edmund Muskie and once ran for governor of Maine. And he had a short-lived partnership in a movie with Joseph Kennedy. "He came out on the short end and hated Kennedy after that," Dave said.

In 1954 Dave joined his parents in Washington and attended Roosevelt High School for his junior year. He'd had enough of the all-boys boarding school and had tasted life in the coed world. Dave's first year at Roosevelt started well. He made the varsity football team and had new friends.

"I was still chasing girls, playing drums and playing football. Studying was not a priority. I managed to pass. It was a period of insanity," Dave said. "Then the Supreme Court made its ruling on desegregation, and the authorities decided the nation's capitol needed to lead the way by desegregating all its high schools literally overnight. At the end of Christmas break, they dumped hundreds of black kids in white schools and white kids in black schools all over the city. It was done precipitously and not handled well, but they had to start somewhere. There were riots and terrible turmoil. Fights broke out at sporting events, and there were 20 to 30 cops on campus for the rest of the year. Everyone became preoccupied with trying to survive. I'd already had a season-ending football injury, when I smashed my foot, and knew I couldn't play sports in the spring. I dropped out of school. I was 16. Logic didn't have much to do with it."

It was February 1955. Through the newspaper classifieds, Dave got a go-fer job at the National Radio Engineering Institute, then one of the leading correspondence schools for electronics and radio.

Working there, he also started taking classes, and the school's research and development caught his interest. It was Dave's first exposure to electronics and technology. Little did he know, at a time when he was more interested in drag racing, that electronics and technology would be his future.

"The technology then had evolved to the later stages of vacuum-tube development, which made it possible to amplify signals for all kinds of uses. It was the predecessor of the transistor. There was also work in solid-state technology. One of the labs was then testing an early color television during the 1955 World Series. The color was terrible, but the concepts were fascinating.

"NREI triggered an interest in engineering and reawakened my interest and curiosity in learning. Between that and gaining some maturity, I realized I needed to finish my education."

Greece

In 1956 Larry Durgin was assigned to Athens for two years, and Dave decided to go. After a year in the workforce, he was ready for a new adventure and some travel.

"We boarded the U.S.S. Independence out of New York. We were at sea a day or two when we were hit by the biggest Atlantic storm in history at the time. Hundred-foot waves tossed the 1,100-foot ship around like a cork. The young and stupid surfaced, and we had a great time. We were the only ones on deck other than crew members who had to be there. It's probably lucky we survived."

That February, Dave entered American Academy, a school founded ten years earlier as a British Army school. It was a small, respected school with about 160 students, many from other countries. The new junior worked hard to catch up. Amin Banani, a Persian teacher, became a friend and mentor. Banani drew Dave into analytical thinking and writing—the fine art of deconstructing a complex idea and reconstructing it in an understandable way. It became a skill that would serve him the rest of his life.

"He was one of the most influential teachers I ever had. He was a history teacher who brought history to life. I'm still interested in history. He probably solidified my interest in learning," Dave said.

As a student at American Academy in Athens, Greece, Dave made up for lost time after dropping out of school in Washington D.C.

After school, students congregated at a tavern called Yorgo's, where the establishment's elderly namesake welcomed his young customers.

By his senior year, Dave was earning straight A's, was class president and captain of the basketball team. He once played against Crown Prince (later King) Constantine of Greece. "Constantine and I were both the starting centers of our teams, but he was starting because he was the Crown Prince, not because he was any good. We got a good early lead before they put in their good center, and we held on to win."

Greece, at that time, was a hot spot. In 1957, during Dave's senior year, the Soviets launched Sputnik, which sent political tremors around the world. The impact was particularly acute in Greece. The Communists, who were challenging Greece's vulnerable democracy, celebrated the Soviet conquest of space and used that historic event to further the cause of communism. Sputnik's impact overseas was much greater than at home.

Another source of tensions was the centuries-old feud between the Greeks and Turks, which erupted into open warfare from time to time on Cyprus, disturbing their coexistence on the island. This conflict was escalating as Dave arrived in Greece and spread to Athens, where riots broke out. Out with his new Greek friends, Dave was caught in the middle of student riots and gained a bit of notoriety after his 1953 Pontiac appeared in a story about the unrest on MovieTone News, showing in American movie theaters.

Mr. Banani assigned Dave the task of writing a paper on the history of the Greeks and Turks in Cyprus. His analysis of the factors leading up to the current hostilities was so insightful that the teacher passed his paper on to American and Greek officials. He traced the unrest in Cyprus to Greek Orthodox Archbishop Makarios, which meant there was little the secular world could do. One point of agreement between the two sides was their sentiment toward the British-run Cypriot government: They both hated the British.

After graduation Dave bequeathed his post at the Greek tavern to incoming seniors, and joined the CIA as a contract employee in Greece. He got the job, Lane recalled, because he had his mother's gift for languages and could speak Greek.

"I was a low-level employee, but I'd gotten to know a lot of people from different walks of life. The agency had people all over the world (my brother was then in Japan and Korea), but they focused on hot spots, and Greece was then a hot spot. There was a strong communist presence and a struggle for the Greek government." Right-wing forces had been fighting Communist rebels for ten years.

"I was undercover, working in a clandestine communications and logistics center at a remote location outside Athens. The agency was then recruiting people who had defected from Eastern Europe and training them as agents to return to their homelands behind the Iron Curtain and spy for us. It was dangerous for them and dangerous for the people working with them." Using his language skills, Dave helped the agent trainers prepare their "students" to use the latest communications equipment, so that they could report back after returning home. Greece had become the CIA's center for such activities.

Dave graduated from high school in 1957.

"Each side knew the other was there, and there were occasional flare-ups. I was sitting with operatives from our side, but I knew people on the other side. There were guys trying to find out who our trainees were, and sometimes the trainees didn't survive. It wasn't open warfare. It was the Cold War, but it had its warm moments. I got paid a regular government salary plus hazardous duty pay, which was in cash in the local currency."

Dave's days as a spook were short-lived. After six months, he returned to the States, passed a grueling screening process at CIA headquarters and became an employee. In February 1958, Dave, now 19, married his high school sweetheart, Patricia McBride, and also decided to continue his education at Capitol Radio Engineering Institute (CREI) in Washington D.C. (now called Capitol College). After six months of full-time work plus night school, the CIA offered him an assignment in Taiwan, which he turned down. He had decided to focus on school. He left the CIA to become a full-time student and part-time teaching assistant.

"I was taking twenty-one hours of classes and teaching thirteen hours. My CREI days were jam packed." For the next three years, he learned, taught, wrote lessons and did some technical writing. Dave would lean on his analytical skills to write lesson plans "deconstructing a subject so students could understand it and reconstructing it into a picture." In January 1961, he had a 4.0 grade point and had earned an associate's degree, Summa Cum Laude.

He got a job offer from Bell Labs and an invitation to interview at Sandia Laboratory in New Mexico. "I'd never heard of Sandia and didn't know anything about New Mexico, but I really liked their recruiter, and it sounded more interesting than Bell Labs.

"As my airplane was on its final approach to Albuquerque, all I saw was a lot of brown and the platted, empty lots that would become Rio Rancho. On February 21, 1961 I walked off the plane for my interview at Sandia, and. it was love at first sight—the open spaces, the pioneering feeling, the air, the sun. Bell Labs in Murray Hill, New Jersey was instantly a distant memory."

2

Sandia

Dave, then 22, joined Sandia Laboratory (it wouldn't become a national lab until 1979) in March 1961 as a technical staff assistant. Sandia, created from Z Division of Los Alamos Laboratory in 1945, had been independent since 1949 and was then managed by AT&T. After World War II, when it seemed the lab might be dismantled, the Cold War gave Sandia a new role.

Sandia had started with a small nuclear stockpile. In 1949 the Soviet Union detonated its first nuclear weapon; as relations deteriorated between the two emerging superpowers, Sandia focused increasingly on engineering and production of nuclear weapons. The arms race was on.

Through the 1950s Sandia augmented its engineering staff and erected new buildings. Demands for increased production pushed the lab from research and development into manufacturing, a new discipline to Sandians. It began field testing and supported work in atmospheric testing at other labs. The pace of weapons development accelerated and was still in high gear when Dave arrived.

The post-war boom in Albuquerque had more than doubled the population (201,189 in 1960) over the previous ten years. New housing subdivisions blanketed the East Mesa, evicting jack rabbits and coyotes. Dave and his bride joined thousands of other young couples in treeless, new neighborhoods served by new shopping centers. Albuquerque had become a city almost overnight, with a freeway system still under construction and the beginnings of a downtown skyline taking shape.

"I went to work at Sandia at a very interesting point in history," Dave said. "The ongoing arms race accelerated into a nuclear test race, and the United States started out way behind. Less than a year later, the Cuban Missile Crisis happened. The following year, our involvement in Viet Nam was accelerating. Sandia had important roles in all of these international crises.

"Sandia was phenomenal. It was neat, challenging work with a lot of smart people, using leading edge technology to address important problems. This was a heady experience for a young technician, and I gained unlimited confidence to take on any technical problem."

Dave's career at Sandia had three phases, which paralleled the lab's response to international issues: Phase 1, nuclear stockpile modernization; Phase 2, nuclear weapon testing; and Phase 3, The McNamara Fence.

The same year Dave joined the lab, he would gain another new title: Dad. After two heartbreaking years of miscarriages and premature babies who died soon after birth, Dave and Patricia adopted two daughters. Dana arrived in 1961. Dianne joined the family in 1962. Both were born on April 18, both prematurely.

Modernizing the Nuclear Stockpile

In January 1960, Soviet Premier Nikita Khrushchev said in a speech that a future war would begin, not with an assault on a nation's borders, but with missile strikes deep in the interior. He also predicted that nuclear weapons and missiles would replace conventional military forces. Khrushchev made missiles a defense priority, and the Russians began deploying large numbers of increasingly sophisticated long-range missiles. In September 1961, the Soviet Union resumed nuclear testing, ending the moratorium established in 1958, and the United States scrambled to catch up

Working in the 7000 Group on nuclear weapons, Dave's primary job early on was to help incorporate new solid-state technology into existing and new nuclear weapons. That meant converting existing fuzing and firing systems, known as firing sets, from electromechanical to smaller and more efficient solid-state technology (electronic components based on the semiconductor). Before the Computer Age, solid-state was a big step up from cumbersome, energy-consuming vacuum-tube technology.

"It was a major conversion. Sandia was ahead of the pack," he said.

The early nuclear devices had a nuclear core surrounded by high explosives, which were in turn surrounded by detonators. To create an implosion on the nuclear core, the detonators had to go off simultaneously, and they relied on a large, high voltage capacitor bank and a vacuum tube switch called a Krytron to deliver the required energy to the detonators. The timing and sequencing of the firing-set functions were controlled by relays and other electromechanical devices.

Dave's early mentor at Sandia was design engineer Bill Price, a Texan with a drawl. Under Price's tutelage, Dave began working on the first solid-state fuzing and firing systems. From 1961 to 1963 he designed and developed firing sets for most of the nuclear weapons in the U.S. inventory. He was also responsible for developing and implementing test programs for the firing sets and overseeing their production at the Bendix Aviation plant in Kansas City—his first experience in manufacturing.

Another mentor, John Souza, showed Dave the ropes in manufacturing operations. As a team, they oversaw the production of about 2,000 firing sets for Sandia. Souza would be one of the designers of an arming, fuzing and firing system produced by Bendix after 1977 and used in the Trident ballistic missiles.

Nuclear Weapons Testing

In fall 1962 Sandians were hard at work modernizing nuclear weapons systems and improving the nation's missile program, when the

Soviet Union attempted to place medium-range missiles in Cuba. This misstep brought the world to the brink of war.

"We were sitting at Sandia wondering where the lab was on the Russian list of missile targets," Dave said. "We believed it was near the top. People were at heightened alert. We were actually assembling weapons inside the Manzano Mountain bunkers (caves hollowed in the mountains for weapon storage). There were nukes and detonators all around you. There was a wartime feeling. Everyone's radios were on. Everyone expected this would blow up. I knew a lab scientist who spent $20,000 building a bomb shelter in the back of his house, and he was renting. It was an intense period of time. When Nikita Khrushchev backed down, it was major. That's the closest we came, in my view, to getting into nuclear war with the Soviet Union."

Khrushchev had lost face. Determined never to show weakness again, the Soviets redoubled their efforts to strengthen their nuclear capabilities, which included accelerating their nuclear testing program and producing more intercontinental and submarine-launched ballistic missiles. At this time the Chinese also joined the nuclear party.

The United States developed an extensive nuclear test program, the Fishbowl series. One part of that, Operation Dominic, involved testing nuclear devices outside the atmosphere. The Air Force's Thor missile was selected for the Dominic tests, and it was reconfigured to carry a payload that included a high-yield nuclear weapon. One of Sandia's tasks in support of Dominic was to provide instrumentation and data recording.

By mid-1962 the redesign work was completed and testing began at Johnston Island, 700 miles from Hawaii. Each test involved a great deal of instrumentation to collect information. Dave had designed and built a preflight performance test complex to make sure that the Thor's payload system and its self-destruct system were ready to go. He supervised the systems' field installation at Johnston Island and Vandenberg Air Force Base and trained Western Electric and military personnel.

At Sandia, Dave designed and developed this pre-launch checkout system
for self-destruct modules.

"To meet critical program deadlines I often went around the bureaucratic structure and dealt directly with vendors instead of going through procurement. It endeared me to certain people and ticked off others," Dave said. "My boss was ready to fire me. His boss appreciated the fact that I'd gotten the job done on time."

The Dominic tests had their problems. Dave's reliable self-destruct system, which set off the payload's high-explosive material without causing a nuclear explosion, was used five times, usually to destroy a missile on its way to space. During the fourth launch, the Thor suffered a liquid oxygen pump failure that damaged the missile and started a fire on the pad. They blew it up on the launch pad, destroying both missile and pad and rendering half the island unusable for a long time.

During the tests, Sandians discovered a little known nuclear effect called Electromagnetic Pulse, or EMP, "On Johnston Island, we were doing exo-atmospheric nuclear testing and inadvertently shut down part of the power grid in Hawaii with an EMP. It revealed a real threat, a newly discovered vulnerability, that hadn't been observed before." Understanding EMP and designing systems to survive it would be Dave's career for the next two decades.

The government needed a replacement for the Thor missile. In less than two months, working around the clock, Sandians designed, built and fired a new, all-purpose rocket, the Strypi. It got its unusual name from a story told by George Dacey, then Sandia's vice president of research, about a British soldier in India who mistook a tiger's tail for a black and yellow snake called a strypi.

Dave's group designed the Strypi, and he was involved in its electronics. "We launched Strypis from Barking Sands in Hawaii. We did a lot of sampling—we'd shoot rockets through clouds. The Strypi was a real workhorse as far as testing."

In 1963 the Limited Test Ban Treaty halted testing in the atmosphere, in space and in the ocean. Sandia for the first time expanded its work into areas other than nuclear weapons development—technologies to monitor nuclear testing, improved space nuclear power systems, development of radiation sensors, and systems to simulate nuclear weapons effects. In laboratory tests, scientists began evaluating the survivability of missile warheads subjected to nuclear explosions in the atmosphere or in space.

The United States needed a monitoring system to detect violations of the test ban treaty. Sandia designed verification technologies, which led in 1963 to the launch of the first Vela satellites to detect nuclear bursts.

The government was also worried about nuclear weapons deployed to Europe for the North Atlantic Treaty Organization (NATO). What if a nuclear device were inadvertently detonated? What if it fell into the wrong hands? Sandia developed the Permissive Action Link (PAL), an electromechanical system designed to prevent accidental or unauthorized detonation. These systems have been refined and improved over the years.

Dave, elevated to technical staff associate, had become one of the lab's leading firing-set designers, and he became involved in the early PALs as one of the designers of the first coded switches and controllers to operate those switches. "We wanted to make it difficult for the bad guy to detonate one of our nuclear weapons, without hindering our ability to do so or reducing the reliability of the system. The early PALs were embedded into the firing sets, which were encapsulated to prevent tampering."

In the same period of time, both the Soviet Union and the United States were developing weapons that could be deployed in space. By the mid-1960s, the Soviets announced a new kind of orbiting satellite armed with a nuclear weapon that could be commanded to re-enter the atmosphere and strike the United States. President John F. Kennedy responded by ordering the development of an anti-satellite weapon. Project 437 was born. Kennedy also began negotiating to ban deployment of weapons of mass destruction in space. After Kennedy's death, President Lyndon Johnson continued both Project 437 and the negotiations. Sandia again had a role to play.

"It was a super-black, highly classified project to develop a missile system capable of shooting down satellites," Dave said. "The program would build on lessons learned from the Dominic test program. The goal was to develop a nuclear-armed missile with a much improved guidance and control system that could be fired at the armed satellite and get close enough to destroy it with a nuclear blast. Guidance, control and tracking systems weren't too accurate in the 1960s, but scientists believed that getting a missile within a mile of the satellite was achievable and could be effective. I was on the project with team members from all over. The objective was a crash program to develop a payload and associated systems."

The Project 437 team was secretly assembled from skilled professionals at Sandia, Bendix, AT&T and other contractors. Dave's responsibility was the design and construction of the pre-launch test system, which was built in the basement of the Bendix plant in Kansas City under tight security. For ten months, Dave spent most of his time in Kansas City. Team members worked day and night, entering and exiting through a hidden entrance. When some of the Bendix unions got wind of the activity, which apparently violated union rules, they picketed the previously hidden entrance. It added one more wrinkle to the project. The team members were exhausted and their families stressed when they completed the project.

In 1965, the day after the system was successfully tested on Johnston Island, President Johnson announced the nation's new capacity to shoot down satellites. After months of hardship and secrecy, Project 437 members weren't happy about the publicity. But Johnson used the anti-satellite weapon as leverage. In 1967 the United States and the Soviet Union signed a treaty that banned weapons of mass destruction in space.

In five years Dave had worked his way into increasingly responsible positions and bigger projects. He was Sandia's top firing set designer, had designed a sophisticated system to test nuclear weapon firing sequence, and had major design responsibilities on Thor's payload and ground test system for the Dominic Series and Project 437. In his spare time, he helped to design some equipment that went on the aircraft involved in atmospheric nuclear testing.

"But it became clear to me that to progress within Sandia I needed more than an associate's degree. I'm not one to ponder a lot. I concluded that going back to school was the right thing to do, and that was it. I went round and round with my bosses. They finally granted me an educational leave but made no guarantees about having a job when I came back."

Back to School

Dave wrapped up his work on multiple programs and entered New Mexico State University's College of Engineering in fall 1965. Dave, Pat, Dana and Dianne moved into student housing, a small, cinderblock cottage with two tiny bedrooms for $64 a month. In the limited time outside school and his part-time job as a teaching assistant, they took the kids to see the animals at the agricultural college's barns, attended some rodeos and drove in their '62 VW bus to the Gila Wilderness to camp. He completed 84 hours of mostly advanced and graduate-level engineering and math courses in two years and graduated Magna Cum Laude in December 1966. At NMSU Dave was president of Eta Kappa Nu, the electrical engineering honor society, and an inductee in Phi Kappa Phi Engineering Honorary and Blue Key, a leadership honorary.

Dave wasn't a typical student or even a typical returning student. "I abhorred homework. It didn't help you learn, it just made you proficient at turning a crank. My approach to studying was to learn why things happen. I'd do reading outside the assignment to understand the basic principles and not do homework. In engineering school, it worked extremely well." Except for the one physics professor who wanted him to turn the crank and gave him one of his few Bs for not turning in homework.

At NMSU he made friends and contacts who would influence him later on. Paul Boulay, an adjunct professor and faculty advisor to Eta Kappa Nu during Dave's tenure as president, was also a manager at BDM, a defense contractor. Living across the street was Don Wunsch, a Ph.D. candidate who was on educational leave from BDM. Wunsch introduced Dave to several BDM executives, and Paul Boulay got Dave an interview at the company's El Paso office, but the only position they could offer was in McLean, Virginia. He had no desire to go back east and turned it down.

Dave has maintained his ties to NMSU, which named him a Centennial Outstanding Alumnus in 1989. He has served on the advisory board of two deans of the College of Engineering and was chairman under Dean Steve Castillo.

Sandia and The McNamara Fence

On graduating from NMSU, Dave looked at some opportunities in private industry but returned to Sandia in January 1967 as a technical staff member. He spent the next year designing and developing micro-electronic circuits and devices for missile payload systems, including precision solid-state oscillators, timers, and firing circuits.

In 1966, Defense Secretary Robert McNamara asked for help in Vietnam. The resulting electronic monitoring system along the Ho Chi Minh Trail became known as the McNamara Fence. Sandia was already working on a device so sensitive it could detect footsteps. It evolved into the COIN (COunter INsurgency) project, one of Sandia's first forays outside the nuclear weapons arena, which launched the lab into sensor-system programs.

Previously detectors like these depended on wires, which weren't practical in the jungles of Vietnam. And they had to be placed by hand. Sandia eliminated the wire and provided a radio link.

"We designed earth penetrating systems disguised as plants for the McNamara Fence. They were thrown out of a plane or helicopter or launched straight down from helicopters. They'd stick in the ground and were self-contained. They'd last up to a year," Dave said. "We designed solid state timers that would trigger transmitters and send information hourly or in one brief pulse monthly, depending on the mission. I designed the solid-state timers and miniature firing sets that were used to launch systems from helicopter-borne launch tubes."

A new area for both Dave and the lab was radiation-hardened components. Because semiconductors are more vulnerable to nuclear radiation and EMP than the old electromechanical devices, the military developed a keen interest in protecting sensitive electronic systems against these nuclear effects. "Suddenly the DOD was developing and funding major programs to evaluate equipment and system vulnerability to radiation effects and EMP," he said.

In the right place at the right time, Dave was becoming knowledgeable in nuclear effects on electronic systems. He was excited to be back in the fold, working on leading-edge projects. He was not excited about the lab's requirement that he pursue a master's degree, a condition of his return.

"It was a situation where I was doing it to check a square, and I wasn't learning a lot. Entrepreneurs are not very patient people. I know few entrepreneurs with MBAs. In my later experience with bigger companies, the MBAs are usually the ones doing the marketing studies. They're smart people and provide valuable research, but they were basically slave. labor. There was a time when I was tempted to get an MBA, but after two years of intense learning, I was ready to focus on new challenges."

Dave was already thinking about business education—not as a student but as a player in the real world.

3

Entrepreneurial Itch

As Dave was undertaking ever more ambitious projects for Sandia, he began to think outside the lab. By late 1967 he had developed a family of precise solid-state oscillators and timers for use in weapon and remote-access, intelligence-collection systems. He believed they had commercial applications in automotive safety systems, industrial controls and security systems, and suggested getting patents. Sandia wasn't interested.

"Technology transfer was not in their vocabulary at that point," Dave said. "I took what I learned and focused on solid-state oscillators and timers—leading edge technologies. They were developed for weapon and intelligence collection systems, but they had lots of applications in the nonmilitary world."

Dave was beginning to chafe at his required attendance at MBA classes under Sandia's Technical Development Program. "Since I am unable to turn off my engineering drive and curiosity at noon, my concentration on academic efforts suffers," he wrote to E. L. Harley on November 15, 1967. That same month, he interviewed with several defense contractors–Gulton Industries, Braddock, Dunn and McDonald (the predecessor of BDM), Douglas Aircraft, Texas Instruments, Honeywell, and EG&G.

Dave was devoting more and more time to developing his product concepts. "I got the idea to go off and commercialize them," he said. "That didn't fit with continuing to work at Sandia. I asked for a waiver, and they said no. I said goodbye. I was hard-headed in those days. I became one of the first entrepreneurs to emerge from Sandia."

Dave's resignation was effective December 8, 1967. The lab wouldn't begin a technology transfer program until 1986; its entrepreneurial leave policy began in 1994.

"I had an entrepreneurial itch. I just wanted to do my own thing. I had no clue what I was getting into. I was 29 years old. I was at least smart enough to know it would be beneficial to jump into some existing entity. At Sandia I had worked with a lot of local contract manufacturing companies to get cables, printed circuit boards and electromechanical assemblies produced. I showed John Wall at Wall Electronics what I was doing and proposed that we work together to commercialize the technology."

He joined Wall Electronics as director of product development. Wall Electronics was one of the few companies of its kind in Albuquerque at the time. During the 1960s the first few technology-related industries had only begun to open operations in the city. Kirtland's research lab had a pioneering laser program that would eventually spawn a local optics industry, but those startups were years away.

In January 1968 Dave applied for patents on the Leslie Oscillator and the Safety-belt Actuated Field Effect Restrained (SAFER) Interlock System.

The object of the SAFER system was to save lives. It used a simple, effective electronic interlock and memory system to prevent the ignition from working if safety belts weren't secured. It was an analog computer, which Dave rolled out long before the auto industry was putting computers in cars. Dave's tenure at Wall Electronics lasted only until October 1968.

"We just banged heads. He was an experienced businessman, and I had no experience but I had very strong views. I suffered from unrealistic expectations. I was inexperienced in negotiating win-win deals. I put that more on my inexperience than on John. I thought John wanted too big a piece of everything I was involved in.

"This is typical even today. The technical person over-values technology and engineering and under-values marketing, sales, finance and infrastructure. Technical people don't understand the importance and complexity of doing market research or business plans. I was a typical technical person."

An Entrepreneur is Born

Late in 1968 Dave started his own company, Product Designs Inc. "Finally I had a platform where I could make all the mistakes in the world. I did the typical entrepreneurial thing—talked friends and family into putting up some money. I raised about $40,000 from outside investors. I invested everything I had."

He leased a 10,000-square-foot building. "As a new entrepreneur, I tended to under-think things and made fairly snap decisions. If I had outsourced the manufacturing, I could have operated in one-third the space with none of the costs of manufacturing equipment and labor."

PDI made solid-state timers, oscillators, power sources and optical sensors. The little company built its own printed circuit boards and did its own manufacturing. At its peak it had ten employees.

"Building printed circuit boards involved chemical plating, a messy process with no value added. I did all my own testing in labs. I'm amazed I didn't try to form my own silicon crystals. It was a self-contained business model. It wasn't an unreasonable approach for a well-capitalized business, but for a start-up, it was just plain stupid. I thought, if I can detonate nuclear weapons, I can do anything. A lot of people coming out of Sandia have the same problem I had. There's a natural tendency for people to want to control things."

PDI added more products: time-delay modules, constant-current modules, low-frequency oscillators, and pulsed voltage dividers, among other things. The products were well received by the auto industry and the manufacturing automation and instrumentation industries. American Motors, the smallest but most innovative of the Big Four automakers, liked the SAFER technology so much that they gave PDI two cars to use as prototypes. Dave had set the family station wagon on fire while testing an early prototype, so this was particularly helpful.

Another of PDI's better products was the Lite-Alert Security System, which relied on some of the earliest optical sensors and solid-state electronics.

"It was our own product—a great product for the time. We used it in our own building. It allowed patrolling security people to shine a flashlight on a photocell that automatically turned on the lights inside the building. It was pretty innovative. It was one of the first sensor-operated security devices."

But Dave didn't understand what it took to launch a product like that. "We didn't know how to find leverage points for sales. Should we go to single access or try for a huge swath of the market? The answer was to join somebody else who already had market access and to make distribution-marketing deals. I had no clue. I was probably calling local security firms. I was also not sure who the customer was."

He was in the same marketing quandary with other PDI products. "I was trying to chase too many markets. A Sandia engineer could give you 20 ideas on how to use a device but not one on how to make money with it. We could wow the technical people but didn't have the marketing savvy or the resources to grow.

"It's important to establish market and application priorities early and use your limited resources to achieve sales and gain traction in the market that will get you to cash-flow breakeven in the shortest time. I also learned that you shouldn't attempt to crack the automotive industry unless you have a lot of money and time."

Dave did figure out that he needed help with sales and recruited an experienced sales representative. Al "Wink" Winklejohn brought some critically needed expertise. Unfortunately, it was too late.

By January the safety of a job was becoming more appealing. Dave made a discreet inquiry about returning to Sandia on Jan. 23. "Unfortunately my current business has received several setbacks and is temporarily stymied because of financial problems. 1969 was <u>not</u> a good year for new companies!" he wrote to Vern Henning, the Sandia human resources manager who had recruited him.

An early catalogue for Product Designs Inc. describes products and features.

"I had peaks and troughs," Dave recalled. "That letter was clearly written during one of my troughs. The setbacks were pretty much all financial and were mostly self-induced. The company didn't have enough capital and did a poor job of cash management."

PDI was over-committed financially, with its large facility and capital equipment, and was woefully undercapitalized, a word Dave didn't understand at the time. "The products were selling, and the volumes were growing, but it wasn't enough to pay the bills. I was constantly trying to raise more money.

"I had a friend who was a vice president of Albuquerque National Bank. I went in and talked to them about what I was doing." The bankers were baffled by Dave's business. "If I'd had a piece of ground or a herd of cattle, they would have provided a loan. But for very early stage high-tech companies, there were zero sources of funding."

The city's banks then were locally owned and relatively small. They were accustomed to mortgages, car loans and capital loans for well established businesses. Bankers here had simply never seen a high-tech startup. Small businesses would complain for years that Albuquerque banks weren't as business savvy as bigger banks in bigger cities.

Dave also tried to snag the interest of Albuquerque's nascent economic development organization (the predecessor of Albuquerque Economic Development Inc.), but its focus was on industrial recruiting outside the state. At the time the business community was giddy over recruiting GE Aircraft Engines and Levi Strauss. Nurturing local start-ups was an idea that wouldn't take hold for decades.

What PDI needed was a venture capitalist or angel (individual) investors, but they didn't exist in Albuquerque in 1968, and there were no networks or support organizations. Albuquerque looked like a city, but its economy was small-town and heavily dependent on Sandia and Kirtland, along with real estate development. Dave could also have used guidance and support.

"Some experienced mentor could have saved me," Dave said. "If I'd had any advice and listened to it, the business would have been gangbusters."

He traveled to Denver and Dallas to meet with investors and investment bankers and found some interest, but he had no credible business plan.

"I told employees, 'We're running out of money.' Everyone wanted this to work. People made a lot of sacrifices. I tried to manage the resources and pushed hard on sales. The bottom line was, there wasn't enough capital to make it work. The difference between this company winding down and being successful was about $50,000."

In 1969, Dave and Pat were pleasantly surprised by her pregnancy. Their third daughter, Patricia, was born in February 1970. In May Dave shut down PDI.

Tech transfer. High-tech startup. Venture financing. Dave was too far ahead of the curve. And he was further encumbered by his own inexperience.

"I made every mistake in the book. It was part of my infallible, young and stupid view of the world. If the young Durgin came to me now, I would throw him out. It would have taken a lot of effort to nurture and mentor that guy."

Marketing

The world's worst advice was, "If you build a better mousetrap, the world will beat a path to your door." One of the most critical, and often brutal, lessons a new entrepreneur has to learn is the importance of marketing.

"At PDI I was totally product driven," Dave said. "I had no ability to do any market research. We were trying to develop and sell too many products into too many different markets. It was a typical lab approach—technology push instead of market pull. It hasn't changed much.

"Marketing and sales, hands down, are the weakest elements of every deal I've been involved with. Engineers and scientists underestimate the difficulty and complexity of somebody else's profession. They think you can just leave a product on the doorstep and people will come by and give you money. You have to clearly identify the end customer: Who, specifically, is going to buy and how do they buy? Once they get that, they're really good at it. It takes some level of detail, analysis, insight and work."

Dave's protégé, entrepreneur-venture capitalist Ron McPhee, described his experience helping a company with sales and marketing. The company's CEO proudly showed Ron a list of ten features he wanted to add to the product. "He needed to have the ten top targets he wanted to sell to," Ron said.

Here are two basic rules:

1. Know your customers and how they buy.

2. Establish market priorities early and use your limited resources to achieve sales that will move cash flow toward break-even.

In conducting primary market research, here are the key questions:

- What is the need for your product or service?
- What user functionality is currently available?
- How do functional requirements vary across markets?
- What is the size of the various markets and segments?
- Who are the lead users? What users will try new technologies and applications before others?
- What are users' buying criteria?
- What are potential future needs?
- Who are current suppliers?

With this information, you can move to specific market research of the early adopters and lead users to identify their product preferences, as well as potential market segments and niches. Additional questions to ask include:

- What potential future applications or products does the lead user desire?
- What are the lead user's unfulfilled product or technology needs?
- What are the potential market entry-access approaches for this group of users?

Next, create a future market profile to include future market size estimate, future players (users, suppliers and advocates), potential product innovation, and other opportunities for new extensions and markets.

4

BDM

ave didn't have the luxury of ruminating on his failed business. He had a family to support. Searching frantically for a job, he rekindled his BDM contacts, and his NMSU friend Don Wunsch got him an interview. BDM's Albuquerque office was hiring.

His interviews with Wunsch and one member of the management team, Bob Buchanan, went well but not his interview with a second member of the management team, Jim Schwarz. Dave and Jim got into a big argument over a subject neither remembers now. "I strongly recommended against hiring him. It's a good thing they didn't listen to me," Jim recalled. The two couldn't imagine then that they would become good friends and even business partners.

On May 18, 1970, Dave became a senior engineer with the firm that became BDM International, an entrepreneurial defense contractor. He'd landed on his feet in what would prove to be the best possible job for him at the time.

BDM started in 1959, when three scientists from Fordham University—Joe Braddock, Bernie Dunn and Dan McDonald—opened a technical services company. (Dunn was a professor; Braddock and McDonald were grad students.) On winning their first contract, to provide analytical support at White Sands Missile Range, the three opened an office in El Paso, Texas, where they cultivated a working relationship with faculty and students at nearby New Mexico State University. In 1966, BDM won a computer-support contract at Sandia and opened a temporary Albuquerque office. When Dave joined the firm, they had taken over the top two floors of the First National Bank Building at San Mateo and Central, then the city's tallest building.

By the late 1980s, BDM would have sales of $500 million and 6,000 employees at 60 locations. The local business press described it as "a high-flying, high-tech, international company."

Government contracting, spurred by Cold War work, had expanded from a small club during the war to an industry its critics would call the Military-Industrial Complex by the 1950s. Sandia alone had 3,500 contractors by 1952.

Some of the city's earliest contractors were the Eidal Manufacturing Co. and Eaton Metal Products Co., operating during the war. The first big defense contractors arrived in the 1960s: Sparton Southwest (switches for the military), Boeing's Aerospace Division, EG&G, and GE Aircraft Engines. In the 1980s others followed: Sperry Flight Systems Defense and Space Systems Division (aircraft flight control systems) and General Dynamics.

Local companies or small companies with local operations also jumped in: Eberline Instruments (1953), CG Electronics (later, Gulton Industries, 1954), SAIC (1969), KTech Corp. (1971), Aquila Technologies (1971), CVI Laser Corp. (1972), L&M Technologies (1972), Applied Technology Associates (1975), and Science & Engineering Associates Inc. (1980).

Nuclear Effects

By this time both the United States and the Soviet Union had sizable nuclear arsenals and were busily testing. Each test delivered more information. Nuclear weapons produce four significant effects: blast, heat, radiation and electromagnetic pulse (EMP). While the blast and heat were relatively predictable, localized effects, radiation and EMP could wreak havoc on entire electronic systems hundreds of miles away. Nuclear detonation in space presented its own issues. The destructive waves of EMP and radiation would eventually attenuate in

Earth's atmosphere, but they could travel unimpeded in the vacuum of outer space.

The Cold War adversaries had to figure out how to protect all their military assets, even if they were nowhere near the point of detonation. The field of nuclear effects was born, along with a booming market for defense contractors. Initially, the work was done by companies with a lone, research-oriented scientist or technologist trying to understand basic nuclear effects. What they lacked was systems-analysis and engineering skills. Here was the real opportunity for companies like BDM.

"In every period of time the government focuses on different programs to address the current threats to our nation," Dave said. "During the 1970s and 1980s, that threat was a nuclear attack by the Soviet Union. All the Department of Defense agencies and branches of the military initiated major programs to evaluate and fix the nuclear vulnerability of all of our military equipment, from planes to missiles, bombs to communications systems. They needed a lot of help developing plans. You go where the money is, and the programs were huge."

BDM was one of the first companies to identify the enormity of the nuclear survivability market. The Albuquerque office focused on aeronautical systems, and the Virginia office focused on Army and communications systems. The core technology expertise and R&D programs were in Albuquerque.

In this new atmosphere of Cold War urgency, the government was initially awarding sole-source contracts. Companies with nuclear-effects expertise and strong analytical skills had the edge, and BDM made it a corporate strategy to become a leader and go after contracts. Despite its small size, BDM was ahead of the curve.

"When you have a major threat and now discover a peripheral threat, like EMP, Congress eats that up," Dave said. "These programs weren't affected by defense cuts. They were ramping up as Vietnam was winding down. The defense establishment always has to justify itself. It's always looking for the cause celebre. This nuclear program made a lot of people's careers, including mine. The cadre of contractors grows to fit the need."

Dave was hired just as BDM established a toehold in this exploding market. The company was expanding its activities from data analysis to systems analysis, systems engineering, research and development, and hardware design. It had moved its headquarters to Virginia, closed its El Paso office, and made Albuquerque its regional center. Albuquerque's management team then included Stan Harrison, a former Sandian hired to expand and grow business with the Air Force; Jim Schwarz, a former Boeing engineer who was an expert in nuclear weapons effects; Bob Buchanan, a Ph.D. electrical engineer; and Don Wunsch, also a Ph.D. electrical engineer and recognized expert on EMP effects on semiconductor devices.

Albuquerque then had few defense contractors. The big dog in the yard, EG&G, called Stan Harrison in and told him not to bother competing. His response was terse and unprintable. In 1970, BDM, with 12 local employees, regularly bid against EG&G, which had 500 local employees. Within a decade, BDM Albuquerque had more than 500 employees and EG&G had 12.

"The Albuquerque office became a center of expertise in nuclear effects and survivability—hot subjects in those days," Dave said. "By this time Joe Braddock had established himself as a thought leader with the Department of Defense, and his insights and contacts helped launch BDM in the emerging nuclear survivability market. From 1970 to my departure in 1979, BDM grew more than 30 percent a year, on average. It was a remarkable period for the company."

Chasing Contracts

Dave and Jim Schwarz didn't encounter each other often until 1971, when BDM teamed with Boeing to pursue the Aeronautical System Vulnerability (ASV) contract, which was to be the Air Force's flagship program for assessing the EMP vulnerability of all strategic aircraft. Boeing's leader on the program, Jim Dicomes, asked Jim and Dave to come to Seattle and work on the proposal.

At Boeing, Dave found engineers working elbow to elbow in noisy bullpens—big, open rooms crammed with desks. Jim was a veteran of the bull pen, but Dave couldn't work that way, so Boeing gave them an office. But because of its open ceiling, the racket was still distracting, so Dave and Jim worked from 4 p.m. to midnight or later, when the plant was quiet. The Boeing-BDM team won the contract and a subsequent follow-on contract and became the nation's experts in protecting airplanes from the effects of EMP.

"The real value I brought to BDM was a cursory knowledge of nuclear effects combined with good analytical and writing skills," Dave said. "I could take a complex technical problem, dissect it into its logical pieces, and develop and document a plan for its resolution."

One of the first assignments on the ASV program was to determine the vulnerability of the B-52's terrain-following radar, which allowed an airplane to fly undetected a few hundred feet above ground.

"Our tests showed that the terrain-following radar would be knocked out by EMP. It got attention at the highest levels of Washington. We recognized, hey, we've got a horse to ride. If EMP could take down a B-52, it meant they had to analyze and test every piece of military equipment there was, starting with the high priority stuff—missiles and planes. It was a wave that swept through the entire military complex."

The Air Force ASV program allowed Boeing and BDM to establish themselves as the nation's leaders in aeronautical system EMP assessment and protection, and they ran with it. Dave, Jim and Boeing's Byron Gage led a Boeing-BDM team that wrote the bibles on the subject (EMP Electronic Analysis Handbook and EMP Electronic Design Handbook). Jim was not only an expert in the field but was one of the first to start worrying about EMP. This and other ground-breaking work established Dave as an expert as well. His new high profile created more business opportunities with defense agencies and military laboratories and commands.

Dave's hardware-related experience developing, testing, and manufacturing electronic systems at Sandia and PDI and his early exposure at Sandia to the field of nuclear effects paid off. He became Test Systems Development Group leader in the Electronic Sciences Department. The unit developed and packaged new instrumentation for both government contracts and commercial sales. He also directed the development of commercial engineering applications for BDM's high-voltage pulse generating and measuring systems. And he expanded BDM's lab operations to include system design, development, and manufacturing capabilities.

"I recall crawling through the guts of a B-1 bomber following huge bundles of wires that can act as an antenna and conduct electromagnetic energy to semiconductors. I'd go meet with customers at places like the Defense Nuclear Agency or Air Force Weapons Laboratory who were just recognizing the magnitude of the nuclear EMP problem and actually help them develop system analysis, system testing and R&D programs. You'd provide a service to your customer while creating business for your company. It was a much more collaborative environment then. Nobody suspected conflicts of interest because everyone was focused on solving a serious problem."

John Darrah, chief scientist at Kirtland's Air Force Weapons Laboratory, was one of the point men for EMP programs in government. "He formed an expert advisory group, and I was the electronics guy. The people who knew about the subject were on a very short list."

Dave also worked on missiles. "We won a major contract from Martin Marietta for the EMP testing and hardening of the MX warhead. The Soviets were believed to have sophisticated missile defense systems. Khruschev had bragged that Russian anti-ICBMs could target a fly."

BDM became a leader in the design, construction and operation of the United States' major EMP test facilities. One of the first was ARES, which tested entire missiles, such as the Minuteman. It was built by EG&G and operated by BDM. Designing, building and operating EMP test facilities would become a major part of BDM's business in Albuquerque for the next two decades.

One of Dave's most memorable projects was The Trestle at Kirtland Air Force Base. The wooden structure would be used to test theories about EMP and to simulate a pulse entering an aircraft. To prevent the distortion of the electromagnetic wave produced by The Trestle, everything, including hardware and bolts, had to be made of wood. McDonnell Douglas led the project, and BDM was a major subcontractor.

"It was a design marvel at the time," Dave said. "We had to be able to park a B-1 or B-2 bomber or even a 747 on it."

Team Building

BDM did so well at selling itself, it was soon scrambling to add expertise. Team building became a priority.

"I got a lot of hiring experience at BDM. We had to hire so many so fast, we'd hire 20 engineers at a time. We got good at it. We'd sit at a table with piles of resumes, and they had to pass three of us. We had some fortuitous planning and some blind luck. We recruited smart young guys out of the Air Force—top notch electronics guys. There was a certain amount of patriotism. It was still not long after the Cuban Missile Crisis.

"We threw a bunch of people together to go do stuff. We learned fast who's good at what. We let people do what they did well. A lot of it was team learning. It became what was probably the top technical team in nuclear-weapons effects in the world. Some of our top people were young officers in the Air Force who knew the subject matter and had real leadership ability. Two of those men were Dave Alexander and Bob Antinone. Dave Alexander became one of the world leaders in radiation-hardened semiconductor devices. Bob spent his career with BDM and its successors, TRW and Northrop Grumman. He has been one of their technical leaders for years."

At that point, Dave and Jim were both group leaders. "I had contracts, and he had people," Jim said. Dave proposed combining the two groups with Jim as group leader and Dave as second in command. Jim would later tell his friend, "Dave, you're really good. You need to have more self-confidence."

BDM subsequently bid three contracts, hoping for one, and landed all three. There is such a thing as too much success: No way could they staff three projects. Dave suggested they discuss it over a drink at El Cid, their favorite after-hours retreat. That night Jim was injured in a car accident, and his recovery took more than a month. Despite being desperately shorthanded, Dave's group managed to complete one project and hold its own on the others. On his return, Jim called the Air Force to apologize.

"They said, 'This is the best job we've ever gotten from BDM. You should stay away more often.' The lesson there is, things don't always have to be done your way," Jim said.

New Partnerships

The industry created by the Cold War grew through the 1970s, fueled by bigger contracts and more money. "Now they had really big contractors involved—the Boeings, the Martin Mariettas, the General Dynamics, the EG&Gs," Dave said. These players and others established Albuquerque outposts, but they were usually more interested in upgrading and selling a plane or a system; they relied on allied companies to provide analysis, and this became the role of smaller companies like BDM and SAIC.

It was an odd competition. The contracts were often so large or the mission so complex that companies teamed up to compete. Yesterday's competitors became today's teammates. They learned each others' strengths and weaknesses, which became useful intelligence in the next contract round if they were on opposite sides. Often competing teams sought out BDM, so BDM conducted its own assessment to determine which was most likely to win.

"The competitors all pretty much knew each other," Dave said. "The same companies had been competing through the 1970s. We knew the people and their backgrounds. It was a much more integrated community."

Dave developed a new skill as troubleshooter. At one point Boeing and BDM were in trouble with the Air Force over an EMP analysis task plan.

"Nobody had analyzed the problem. I said I'd take a shot at it. I took the problem apart and put it back together and wrote a new task statement that made everything crystal clear. It was an analytical exercise and a writing exercise. Those skills work for you in writing proposals. You can have a lot of brilliant analytical and technical people who can't write squat. You look at the big picture and break it down. These skills have been the underpinning of everything I've done."

Dave's new work plan earned praise from all the parties and, essentially, saved the contract. His high-school training with Mr. Banani paid off.

"I became the go-to guy on work with Air Force customers. We had a lot of work with Boeing. I became good at conceptualizing solutions and writing them down—how to attack a problem, how to get it done."

Management Team

In time Dave became heavily involved in developing proposals and going after new business. He discovered that building business in a small, entrepreneurial company wasn't unlike running PDI. "Each one was a new business, and each had a start-up environment. The difference was the financial underpinning. I came from having no clue at PDI to growing up through BDM." In the process of writing detailed plans of everything that had to be done on a project, he gained the skills and insight to write a business plan and prepare detailed budgets.

Dave continued moving up, becoming manager of the Electronic Vulnerability Department in 1975 and director of Systems Engineering and Weapon Effects the same year. In 1976, Dave took over Jim's EMP group, and Jim took over the laser group.

Dave rose through the ranks at BDM to become a member of the executive team.

In 1976 the four-man executive team formed that became something of a legend in Albuquerque business. The members were Dave Bailey, who was overall manager; Dick McGuire; Dave and Jim.

"The four guys were very different. Each had some strong skill sets," Dave said. "Jim Schwarz is an operational animal—he's good at it, and he likes it. I was good at conceptualizing and winning programs. Dick was the marketing and sales guy. Bailey was a brilliant guy. He was good at getting the most out of this leadership team."

"Bailey was the smartest guy I ever knew," Jim said. "He was a big guy, with big hands. He had a management style that could adapt to the needs of the person. And he could keep meddling from BDM's Washington office to a minimum. If I came into his office with an idea, Bailey would either say, 'You're right,' or 'You're wrong, and here's why.' Bailey could also drink any of us under the table. Bailey never sold anything; his ability was to manage. I never met anybody else like that."

On their watch, the Albuquerque operation grew to about 1,200 employees with more than $50 million in contracts in system analysis, system engineering, research and development, system and subsystem testing, and system operational test and evaluation. Customers included Sandia, Air Force, Army, Navy, the Defense Nuclear Agency, Harry Diamond Laboratories, Air Force Weapons Laboratory, Naval Research Laboratory, TRW, Boeing, and Martin Marietta. The nuclear effects-related business, run by Jim Schwarz, was large, but the operational test and evaluation business, run by Dick McGuire, was larger. BDM was recognized as a leader in both communities.

This BDM management team worked hard and played hard. Logging 24 to 48 hours straight wasn't unusual, nor was an occasional eight-hour lunch. Their drinking sessions, at watering holes like as El Cid and Cervantes, became legendary.

Dave became assistant vice president of Systems Engineering in 1977 and vice president a year later. BDM was booming. Dave managed more than 200 people, ran the R&D Laboratory and was responsible for a multi-million dollar contract portfolio.

The frequent travel and long hours that contributed to Dave's business success had a price. In 1978 his first marriage ended.

He met his second wife at BDM. Eilene Prewitt, whose roots are in western New Mexico in the town of the same name, had joined BDM during its high-growth years to work in program control (helping program managers track expenditures against specific government contracts). They married on June 30, 1978. Their differences in style and temperament inspired office bets on the duration of their marriage. Jim Schwarz gave them six months. At this writing, they beat that prediction by thirty years.

"Our honeymoon was in Hawaii, and I decided to teach this non-swimmer how to snorkel," Dave said. "Bad move! She wouldn't let go of my hand and broke my wrist on some coral as she thrashed about.

To her credit, she became a certified scuba diver two years later."

Eilene had two children, son Lewie and adopted daughter Erica, her niece.

CEO Earl Williams, an Alabama native who had joined BDM in 1962, made it clear that he frowned on having a husband and wife in the same operation. It wasn't company policy at the time; Williams was applying his own standard to his newest vice president. Dave vividly recalls meeting Williams in the Presidential Suite at the AMFAC (now Wyndham) Hotel by the Albuquerque airport. Williams tried to explain the logic of his new interpretation of BDM's employee intermarriage policy, which he applied only to company officers.

"I didn't take it well," Dave said. "For all intents and purposes, he was asking me to fire my wife."

Dave was then responsible for all marketing and management activities in a broad technical area that accounted for $7.3 million in R&D contracts. The business growth rate in his unit had exceeded 30 percent per year for the previous five years and zoomed to 46 percent in 1977. But after reflecting on the confrontation with Williams and the pressure on his new marriage, Dave decided to look at new career opportunities.

BDM was still entrepreneurial but moving toward a more formal, centralized corporate structure, with more procedures and policies. "I recall a conversation at the time that the more successful we were, the more burdened we were with formalities. Fortunately we had built a great team, so the distraction wasn't fatal," he said.

Dave got a call from a headhunter that led to a job offer. Bailey reluctantly announced Dave's resignation on March 20, 1979.

Earl Williams took BDM public the following year, and BDM continued to grow. By 1988 BDM Albuquerque accounted for 40 percent of the company's business. Its massive operation near the Albuquerque airport employed 800 people, for an annual payroll of more than $28 million.

BDM was enjoying the last of the big-spending Reagan years,

just before the collapse of communism in Eastern Europe. In 1988 it was acquired by Ford Aerospace. That wasn't a good fit, and Ford sold BDM in 1990 to the Carlyle Group, a Washington-based merchant banking firm, which sold it in 1997 to TRW. In 2002 TRW was itself acquired by Northrop Grumman. Some of the original BDM Albuquerque nuclear survivability team members are still with the company's successor, but Dave's team, for the most part, moved on.

BDM during its heyday was an important presence in Albuquerque. Besides its big payroll, the entrepreneurial climate encouraged new business development. It became a spawning ground for such new enterprises as SBS Engineering, Los Alamos Technical Associates, and the company Dave and Jim Schwarz would start in 1988. Jim left the company in 1987; Bailey left in 1989.

The 10X Rule

Most successful professional-services firms selling to the government, and specifically to the Department of Defense, develop relationships at several levels within each customer organization. They do this to gain an in-depth understanding of the threat to which they are responding and the specific mission of each organizational entity.

Because internal communications within these organizations are typically poor, the contractors who can understand and communicate the big picture can be invaluable in helping each organization develop and implement needed programs. This also benefits the contractor by providing a strong position for both sole source and competitive procurements.

"Dan McDonald had what he called his 10X rule: Know ten times as much about your customer's needs as they do," Dave said. "That way you bring tremendous value to the customer when it comes to designing programs to accomplish their mission. Selling professional services is not like selling hardware off the shelf. Cost is not the primary consideration but the ability to do the job.

"The most successful professional services companies— SAIC, BDM, Booz Allen Hamilton, TRW, to name a few— established relationships with everyone from generals to grunts and did continuous research to understand what was driving the defense establishment at any particular time.

"Several of these organizations had senior executives on major policy making or policy reviewing bodies, such as the Defense Science Board or military advisory boards. Over the years, Joe Braddock, Dan McDonald and a number of BDM's retired generals served in such capacities and provided valuable insights to the company. Needless to say, their contributions to these boards were highly valued by senior military and DoD officials, so it was a fair two-way street."

Dave calls this approach "total immersion" marketing. "Immerse yourself in your customer's world so that you can bring real value because of your in-depth understanding of the threat, the strategy and each organization's role in developing end executing the tactics. This approach works for even the most technical tasks in R&D projects."

5

Booz Allen Hamilton

After Earl Williams threw down the gauntlet at BDM, Dave accepted a headhunter's invitation to come to Washington D.C. There he met with the CEO and several senior executives of Booz Allen Hamilton, the venerable management consulting firm. BAH wanted to enter the rapidly growing nuclear survivability market and needed someone to start a business for them.

During the courtship that followed, Dave attended the company's 1978 Christmas party and had long discussions with the management team, during which he roughed out a business plan. Booz Allen subsequently offered Dave a position as vice president and partner, and he accepted. He joined the firm in March 1979 at age 40.

It was a big move up, but it meant leaving Albuquerque. Dave, Eilene and their blended family of her two children and Dianne, one of Dave's three daughters, moved to Vienna, Virginia. Dave left reluctantly, but he knew he'd be back. In fact, he quickly opened a Booz Allen office in Albuquerque to pursue major defense programs with the Air Force.

Unlike the small, aggressive BDM, Booz Allen Hamilton was large and entrenched. Edwin Booz in 1914 had conceived the idea of providing objective, outside expertise to companies and in the process of founding his company, launched the new profession of management consulting. Based in New York City, BAH in 1979 was privately owned by its 120 partners. The company's government business was headquartered in Bethesda, Maryland. Dave, as head of the new Nuclear Technology Practice, was charged with building a technology consulting business with key Department of Defense organizations and defense contractors.

"It was an entrepreneurial environment but within a corporate structure—a partnership—that was ideal for entrepreneurial people," Dave said. "Each partner is an entrepreneur running one or more businesses as an owner. I thrived there."

During his time with Booz Allen Hamilton (1979 to 1990), Dave rose through the ranks to become senior partner and a member of the firm's Operating Council.

Nuclear survivability would be a major issue through the 1980s. Communist bloc military forces outnumbered those of the western nations, and NATO countries relied on nuclear weapons to deter the Soviet Union from invading Western Europe. But the weapons' high cost made production of large quantities prohibitive, so the military had to ensure that the existing weapons could outlast those of the enemy.

Business Plan

By July 20 Dave had a business plan. He developed concepts and strategies in a briefing format that included graphics, flow charts and critical-path analysis. He mapped out how to proceed and set priorities.

By habit, he broke a big subject into understandable segments by answering questions: Why nuclear technology? What is nuclear technology? Where is the business centered? He identified a business development strategy, specifying which agencies would be targeted, along with the corresponding efforts.

He outlined the first year's activities:

- First month: Assess and package corporate capability;
- First and second month: Develop strategy and prepare plan;
- Second through sixth months: Implement plan, contact customers, conduct briefings;
- Sixth through twelfth months: Follow-up and recruit key personnel.

He projected contracts to be in force within a few months. This included a marketing target analysis of specific agencies, as well as sizing up the competition and Booz Allen's competitive position. (One of the targets was Boeing, and BDM would be a competitor.) He described the value of prospects, action necessary, the ratio of investment to payoff, and the estimated time. He identified key hires and estimated their near-term billability.

"I was a kid in a candy store," he said. "They didn't change anything in my plan." From the beginning, Dave made Albuquerque a business center and opened an office here focused on Air Force Weapons Laboratory, Air Force Test and Evaluation Center, Department of Energy, Sandia and Defense Nuclear Agency. Traveling back and forth, he would accumulate nearly a million frequent-flier miles between Albuquerque and Washington D.C.

Booz Allen had well established internal systems for monitoring and tracking. Every business entity had a plan for each year. "By the time I got to Booz Allen, my own knowledge of planning had grown. My approach to things fit well. PDI was, at best, back-of-the-envelope stuff. At BDM I did more planning. Booz Allen was more formal. At every level I was learning. I also learned to set priorities."

During the first year, Booz Allen invested about $115,000 in the Nuclear Technology Practice, which was less than Dave's estimate of $157,000. It generated sales of more than $230,000, produced 15 to 20 qualification packages and 14 major briefings, and won all the procurements decided in the period. The practice also hired 86 percent of the needed professionals.

"I had total autonomy," Dave said. "I had all the clout to access resources. It was a phenomenal platform for growing a business. I basically paid for myself in six months. I was a cheap date as an entrepreneur. It amazed them. They didn't plan for that."

Dave's technical reputation gave him access to key clients, but he had no contracts. Former colleagues allowed him to piggyback on their contracts. "They didn't feel threatened. They allowed me to use their contract to do work. It allowed us to get funded for sole-source work. Nine months later, Booz Allen got its first sole source contract. I used that to build capacity and go after bigger programs and build more capacity and go after even bigger programs."

Dave won his first contract from the Defense Nuclear Agency

within 90 days. In less than a year he won his first million-dollar contract from the same agency. Dave and his growing team continued to win major contracts with the DNA, the Army and the Air Force. A high point was a $5 million, multi-year contract with the Air Force Operational Test and Evaluation Center at Kirtland Air Force Base.

"You have to do a lot of homework before the request for proposals ever comes out. We worked on this for a year. It became the business backbone for the Albuquerque office. We were a rousing success."

Business building was considerably eased by having a savvy assistant.

"Senior Vice President Ken Mundell gave me his secretary because she knew the company. Ellie Borzilleri was amazingly knowledgeable. She could take a thing dictated electronically, and it would come out perfect. I could put out proposals, briefings. I could be incredibly responsive. She was more than a secretary. She was organized in a way that was practical, and she kept me organized. It was a key engine for the years I was there."

Albuquerque Office

The second person Dave hired was Bill Herman, who was fairly typical of other team members. Bill had served 10 years in the Air Force, primarily with Air Force Weapons Laboratory at Kirtland. He had worked briefly in private industry and for government when he answered an ad and joined Booz Allen in 1979 as a senior associate. He would work for the company and Dave for ten years.

Bill knew nothing about Booz Allen but soon learned it was a "very old school consulting company," Bill said. "Dave hired me to start the Albuquerque office to do projects in nuclear survivability." Bill's background recommended him; Air Force Weapons Lab was a center for nuclear survivability research, and he had worked closely with three national laboratories.

"We started building a staff in Albuquerque focused on Air

Force clients and the Defense Nuclear Agency. Dave began to hire people in the Bethesda office focused on the Army and the Defense Nuclear Agency." The latter, then, had a site in Albuquerque on the old Sandia Base inside Kirtland to support underground nuclear-weapon testing.

"I rented space on Eubank, which Dave hated," Bill recalled. It was conveniently located near the base but didn't fit Booz Allen's upscale image. "They were very conscious of being a consultant to CEOs. It was a high-end firm."

Bill moved the operation to a more prestigious address near the airport. The location may have improved, but the Albuquerque team didn't necessarily look the part. Bill remembers that Booz Allen executives were shocked to see a photograph of their Albuquerque employees—not a tie in the group.

"Albuquerque, even then, was a casual place," Bill said. "In Bethesda, everybody looked like bankers. They'd put on a jacket to go to the men's room. We were told to always wear suits of natural fiber." In other words, no polyester. Dave, he recalled, always dressed extremely well.

Some of the company's commercial-sector partners initially viewed their Booz Allen counterparts in government business as second-class citizens. This attitude faded quickly as Dave and others rapidly grew large, profitable businesses. One of Dave's allies in government business became the company's CEO in the late 1980s, establishing a tradition that would hold during the tenures of three CEOs over two decades as they grew a $4.7 billion business.

Dave grew his organization to 125 people in less than five years. "Because we were selling services, people were the base, and a big part of the job was recruiting," Dave said. "It's critical that your early hires are good hires. I brought in people I already had some history with and stole a few from BDM."

Dave and Bill hired a senior management team that was already in the nuclear survivability business. After that, they looked for a background in nuclear weapons effects and hired a number of people with a broad background in engineering, physics and aerospace. Then they taught them the consulting business.

"It was the kind of business where people moved around, and contractors would hire from one another," Bill said. "Dave taught me what talents to look for beyond what's on a resume. He did a good job of hiring. You need to get a real understanding of whether they really have the skills they say they do. You need to understand how they think, how they solve problems, how they write. In a communications business (like consulting), everything is either oral or written. If their communications skills aren't good, you'll fail. Communications skills are almost as important as technical skills. In a consulting business, it's all about the people. Nothing else you have has value for the customers or investors."

Booz Allen didn't hire people until they were needed, so they didn't have employees sitting with unbillable hours. "We'd get reports every two weeks on how much of everyone's time was being billed," Bill said. "That business is about selling people's time. Otherwise your costs would be too high. I spent a lot of time on time billed."

The work itself involved engineering research or studies. "Dave always thought about a technique to solve problems that we could make into a unique Booz Allen method of delivering solutions, a trademarked approach to problem solving—productizing your approach to problem solving. A lot of times, the client would have to fight for funding for the things we were recommending. If a proposal was well founded and led to good results, it usually meant growth in their budget."

Like BDM, Booz Allen also teamed with other organizations to win contracts.

"There's a whole mating dance if you need a partner," Bill said. "Maybe they have a closer relationship with a customer or a unique skill. You were always selling your expertise. You interviewed the customer and tried to understand what they were looking for. I may know everything I needed to know, but if I bring in X, it helps sell my expertise. Dave was very good at it. We had a very high success rate.

"I learned a lot from Dave. He's a very strategic thinker. He's always been a mentor. Dave is much more comfortable with the strategic part of the operation than with management. He enjoyed strategizing. He was always thinking a step ahead of everyone else. When you're going to do a project for the customer, you had to step back and look at the big picture—not just what they thought was important."

The offices in both Maryland and Albuquerque grew rapidly, leading to the formation of Booz Allen's Defense and Energy Technology Division, which Dave managed. Subsequently, Dave became a senior partner and, in 1986, a member of the firm's prestigious Operating Council, the forum for discussing issues of importance to the partnership.

Back to Albuquerque

By 1985 Dave was presiding over a much larger organization, and the administrative and personnel responsibilities were growing tiresome, and the attractions of the Beltway paled. He returned to New Mexico that year and began managing his division from the Albuquerque office. He subsequently became Western Region Managing Partner of Booz Allen's government and technology consulting business to justify living in the West.

"I think he was already beginning to look to his future," Bill said. "In the mid-1980s government contracting changed dramatically. It wasn't as much fun as it used to be. The Competition In Contracting Act changed the rules of the game. It was no longer who had the best proposal but who was the cheapest." Each contractor tried to prove its hours were the longest and the lowest paid. "It changed the way we did things."

Dave felt the first strains with Booz Allen. In his performance review in 1985, a superior wrote: "Dave has been successful in recruiting a superior cadre of top-notch professionals... Dave has set up management systems which foster the development of senior staff, such as his marketing management approach and the establishment of marketing action groups." But the superior preferred to develop managers from the bottom up, while Dave wanted to hire heavy hitters (just as he had been hired).

One of his mistakes in that period was taking on Booz Allen's troubled Energy Group. Dave managed to win a multi-million dollar procurement with the Electric Power Research Institute, the research arm of the electric utility industry. But the Energy Group also had contracts with DOE at a time when energy companies were under fire from the media for having both government and commercial work. On top of that, the 1986 tax revision doomed alternative energy, and the Energy Group itself was simply dysfunctional and unmanageable.

"It wasn't one of my smarter moves," Dave said. "I stabilized it. I recruited a guy to manage it, and it was one of the bigger recruiting mistakes I made. It wasn't fixable, and we shut it down. In hindsight this experience was probably good for me. I took on the challenge because I was asked to and my arrogance fueled by recent successes got me in trouble. I had no personal basis to understand the industry and no relationships with people who could provide personnel referrals. I was shooting blind. Another lesson learned!"

By 1987 Dave was leading assignments in nuclear and conventional survivability for the Defense Nuclear Agency, the Air Force Operational Test and Evaluation Center, the Army's Harry Diamond Laboratories, and the joint-service Survivability-Vulnerability Information Analysis Center. That year Congress forced the Star Wars project to scale down, but expenditures in survivability research increased.

What if we win?

Dave was beginning to see the good times ending.

"Pretty much all through the 1980s, I worked on a lot of classified programs and had access to intelligence. We could see the disintegration of the Soviet Union. Long before the fall of the Berlin

Wall, I had discussed it with people: The Soviet Union will fall apart. What does that mean for our business?

"The defense establishment is threat driven. For 50-plus years, it was driven by the nuclear threat from the Soviet Union. If the threat wasn't there, what were the next forces to drive the defense establishment? Now it's the terrorist threat. Frequently they make up threats so they can be driven where they want to go. There was a lot of what-if conversation.

"Tens of trillions of dollars were spent responding to the nuclear threat. We had developed technology aimed at responding to that threat. We built smarter satellites to spy on them, better missiles to fire at them. The United States then spent about $140 billion a year on R&D, but less than ten percent of that technology ever benefited the commercial market. How do you move some of that investment to the private sector?

"That was the germ. It bubbled around. Where should this occur? New Mexico was the logical place to do something because of its history during the nuclear age and the huge technology assets that had grown here over the previous 50 or 60 years."

When Dave raised the possibility of technology commercialization businesses within Booz Allen, the response was lukewarm. The partners thought the concept was premature or too far out.

"I started to brainstorm with friends and colleagues in New Mexico, including Jim Schwarz. Out of that came the concept of a technology commercialization company. But when we'd go out and pitch it, people would say, what in hell is that? We weren't the only ones thinking about this. Many knew that if peace broke out, New Mexico could be in serious trouble."

In 1989 Booz Allen introduced a new retirement policy, which granted early retirement to employees who had served as partners for ten years. Dave hit the milestone that year. "I told them I would retire in March 1990, one year. My group was then engaged in competitions to retain all of our major contracts. I said I wouldn't leave until this process was wrapped up." His unit won all its recompetes, leaving the company a $200 million backlog in contracts. He also left an established senior management team he had developed, including Bill Herman, Lin Albright and George Greenleaf, and a new hire, Foster Rich.

"I like to build a company, but I don't enjoy running one. You do what you do well," Dave said.

Booz Allen would grow to employ more than 19,000 employees on six continents and post annual sales of more than $4 billion.

Bill Herman left Booz Allen in 1989 to work for SEA in Albuquerque and three years later got out of the survivability business. "In 1989 the Berlin Wall came down, and a lot of the work I was doing became much less important," he said. At the time, he had an opportunity to join a software company and changed careers at age 51. In 1996 he started his own company, Tekworks, a consulting firm that did customized software development for government and commercial customers. It was acquired by Altiris, which was subsequently acquired by Symantec.

"I learned the whole consulting business from Dave and Booz Allen," Bill said. "Dave was really my mentor in the business world, and he was a very good teacher. I credit him with the knowledge I had to start a business later. He taught me how to think about business—how to take the strategic view, see the big picture, how to keep track of finances, how to track projects. I learned about hiring people, about marketing and writing proposals, building relations with people in government and with customers, how to give value to the customer so they would continue to hire you. He liked mentoring. He held me accountable."

Dave and other experienced business people say that people are the single most important element of a company. "It's a hard process, and there's nothing more important that you do in building a business," Dave said. "It's not a matter of a good or bad person, but the right person."

Beginning at BDM, Dave learned that competent human resource professionals can make a difficult process easier.

"HR skills don't come naturally to somebody of my background. People who don't have that ability will fail unless they find somebody who does. It's a tough problem. I learned this the hard way at BDM, where the company's managers would sit around a conference table sorting through stacks of resumes trying to winnow them down to those worthy of our precious time for interviews. Since then, I have found and regularly used outstanding HR consultants. They'll eliminate 80 percent of the turkeys so you don't waste your time."

Once the field is narrowed, and serious interviewing begins, decisions should involve more than one person.

"A diversity of input in evaluation is important. Managers shouldn't rely solely on themselves to hire, no matter how experienced they are. When you have people who understand the requirements of the job, they come at it from a different angle. You should have three or four people involved in that interview and screening process, and you should have somebody who's not just another you. At BDM, we developed a tag-team approach to interviewing in which everyone had a specific role."

Dave's protégé, entrepreneur Paul Short, recommends a process in which one employee at a time interviews the candidate. At the end of the day, they compare notes. "If you hear a consistent story, that's a good sign," Paul said. "If you hear different answers to the same question, it's not. It may also mean they treat a grunt and a manager differently. That's a red flag."

Paul also employs some behavioral interview techniques: "Tell me about a time when…" to get a sense of how the candidate works and plays with others.

Dave recommends evaluating a candidate for the present and the future.

"You have to have a clear understanding of what you're hiring for, and it's not just the job description. You're looking for people who can do what you need done right now but have the potential to grow and contribute down the road."

He believes in references—official and unofficial. "References from people you trust are huge. All my better hires were referrals."

And everybody should be on the same page. "It's important to make sure your expectations and the prospective hire's expectations are in line. If you have a clash of expectations from day one, you don't ever get over that. You need the proper skill set and a real intersection of expectations."

In the same vein, Dave learned that the old adage about a bad apple is true.

"If you get somebody who's a disruptive force, you have to get rid of them. I don't believe in keeping people like this just because their skills are good. This is easier to do in a small company. Large companies will tell you 14 reasons why you can't do it because you'll get sued.

"Another HR problem is the self-absorbed individual with no sensitivity to people. No matter how bright or talented, somebody like this in a management position is bad news."

6

Quatro Corporation

The city Dave intended to be home to his new technology commercialization business in 1989 was considerably more evolved than it was in the late 1960s, during PDI's short life.

The New Albuquerque

Albuquerque's long dependence on Sandia, Kirtland and government contractors began to shift in the 1970s. The Singer Company opened its Friden Division in Albuquerque and soon employed 1,300 people building business machines; when Singer closed in 1976, Digital Equipment Corporation moved into the plant and began manufacturing computer workstations and components. A former Air Force engineer, H. Edward Roberts, developed the first practical, affordable home computer, the Altair 880. His company, MITS Inc., dominated the new industry in the mid-1970s. (Dave, then at BDM, bought stock in MITS.) In 1975 Roberts hired two young men to write software: Paul Allen and Bill Gates, who started Microsoft in Albuquerque.

Roberts sold his company in 1977 to Pertec. Gates and Allen moved Microsoft to Seattle in 1978, setting off a negative Albuquerque urban legend to the effect that the city lost Microsoft because banks didn't support it. The reality was that the two youthful Microsoft geniuses were originally from Seattle. They were in Albuquerque only because of MITS. And banks here had little experience with tech startups.

By then the first wave of electronics companies had begun exiting California in search of lower costs, bigger labor pools and room to grow. GTE Lenkurt chose Albuquerque in 1971, followed by Motorola. In the 1980s a second wave delivered Intel, Signetics, Ethicon, Sperry, Olympus, and Honeywell.

After returning to New Mexico to head Booz Allen's western office, Dave began networking to understand the changing business climate in New Mexico. One of the first people he met was Ray Radosevich, then dean of the University of New Mexico's Anderson Schools of Management. Ray had also seen the potential of tech transfer.

"The feds were spending upwards of $2 billion here, and there was no history of consequential spinoffs," Ray said. "We were a poor state with political clout and a lot of technology."

With a grant from the National Science Foundation Ray had founded the New Mexico Technological Innovation Program (TIP) in 1980 as an independent nonprofit with the goal of helping companies. In return for services, TIP would be paid in stock. For the next five years, TIP helped create 50 small companies—21 based on lab technology, 11 on university technology and 18 from individual inventors—and raised $31.9 million in seed funding. The program's chairman was Gene Stark, who was Industrial Initiatives Officer at Los Alamos and chairman of the Federal Laboratory Consortium for Technology Transfer. By 1988 half the companies were still operating.

It was a start, but New Mexico's labs and universities weren't ready to support tech transfer. Administrators objected to program costs and predicted a brain drain if their most creative scientists departed to commercialize their devices.

"Everything Ray recommended, we needed, but there was only one Ray," said Chuck Wellborn, an attorney working with startups. "He was the one guy doing all the right things. If we'd done all the things Ray wanted done in the 1980s, we'd be in a lot different place today."

Ray was also involved, in the early 1980s, with the New Mexico

Entrepreneurs Association. The informal group was a Who's Who of early entrepreneurs, including Gary Seawright, Jeff Bullington, Joe Evans, Ron Lohrding, John Barclay, Graham Gurr, Terry Koontz, John Milewski, Dick Meyer, Red and Linda McLellan, Charles Stein, Gary Smith, Larry Stolarczyk, Leland Trayler, Waneta Tuttle, Paul Vosburgh, Gene Watson, and Ebtisam Wilkins. Dave was a member or board member at different times.

The idea was to provide support to budding entrepreneurs and encouragement to lab and university employees who might become entrepreneurs, Ray recalled.

"The thought was that those who succeeded and even those who died trying would have valuable insights to share," Ray said.

Chuck Wellborn, who served on the board, saw the association as an important step. "It's surprising now what a buzz there was. Many of us could see the possibilities, but we didn't know how to move things along. We didn't have the mix of entrepreneurs and venture capital we needed, but we were this close." When Chuck and Dave met, "I thought Dave had the right combination of technical and business skills to make good things happen."

Another group that formed in the same period was Biomedical Tuesday, which evolved into the New Mexico Biotechnology and Biomedical Association (now called NMBio). Organized by biomed-biotech pioneers Waneta Tuttle and Ross Robinson along with Chuck Wellborn, Biomedical Tuesday provided a place for entrepreneurs, researchers, inventors and investors to meet and talk.

Albuquerque was beginning to see itself as something other than a government town, but it was still missing some critical pieces—venture capital and experienced business managers.

On a national level, the fall of the Berlin Wall heralded the end of the Cold War. As defense budgets shrank, along with the defense industry and its jobs, the logical next step—and New Mexico anxiously awaited a next step—was to try and find peaceful uses for technology produced during the Cold War and the defense-industry brain trust that had created it. In the face of new challenges from Japan to keep the nation competitive, there was a new sense of urgency.

Congress tried to jump-start the process with the Federal Technology Transfer Act of 1986. It handed federal lab scientists and engineers the responsibility of transferring their technology and even made it part of their performance evaluations. It provided for royalty sharing between inventors and labs and allowed labs to forge licensing agreements with companies, large and small.

New Enterprise

Technology commercialization had long been Dave's goal, and now the ball was rolling. Dave's old friend Jim Schwarz left BDM in 1987. Jim recalled, "I was thinking I would retire. Dave got on my case. 'We gotta work on tech transfer.' What's that? What do you mean 'we?'

"Dave said, 'I'll keep working at Booz Allen. You start the company. I'll come over when it's up and running.' I was cruelly manipulated, but it was done so cleverly I thought it was my idea."

Rich Hoke, who would join later, recalled: "The legend is that Dave and Jim hatched the company over a bottle of Black Velvet."

Wanting to reprise the old magic at BDM, they involved Dave Bailey, who in turn recommended George Rhodes, a physical chemist with five patents and 25 years' experience with BDM, the Department of Energy and the Department of Defense.

"We had four principals, or cuatro," Dave said. "Jim, who didn't speak Spanish, filed the incorporation papers, and it came out 'Quatro.'"

The name stuck. Quatro was incorporated in November 1988 and began operations in January 1989 as a tenant in the New Mexico Business Innovation Center, the city's business incubator. Three partners invested $180,000 to capitalize the company—Dave, $90,000; Bailey, $60,000; and Jim, $30,000. The amounts were based on who would spend the most sweat equity during Quatro's first year. Dave took early retirement and began wrapping up his work at Booz Allen.

Meanwhile, Jim and George were setting up the company's operations and beginning to look for business.

Talking the Talk

Quatro was the first New Mexico company to get on the technology transfer bandwagon. What the partners didn't realize was that they would have to push that wagon uphill for years.

Quatro faced three challenges. First, the business climate in Albuquerque and the state had improved since Dave's PDI days, but it still wasn't fertile ground for startups. The long dependence on federal funding created an indifferent atmosphere for entrepreneurs. "Nobody wanted to take risks," Dave said. "How do you incorporate risk taking into a risk-averse culture? It was a big problem."

Second, the labs themselves were still reluctant. The 1986 tech-transfer legislation had exempted weapons labs, and an executive order from President Ronald Reagan actually unraveled the intent of Congress by providing rights to large companies while undermining the position of small companies. Sandia started a tech transfer program, but it was window dressing.

"Neither (Sandia director) Al Narath nor Sandia's first tech transfer czar, Jerry Yonas, was really supportive of the idea. They had a core mission and didn't want to be deterred," Dave said. "There were no policies—nothing in the fabric of Sandia that was entrepreneurial. There were also a lot of people in Congress who were not supportive of tech transfer. Sandia didn't want to tick off key members of Congress or their sponsors at DOE and risk its multi-billion-dollar budget. The fact that tech transfer was hard was always an excuse for not doing anything."

The state's universities, like the labs, were preoccupied with their own missions and oblivious to the possibilities of commercializing faculty inventions. With a seemingly bottomless well of federal money, there was no motivation for labs or universities to be entrepreneurial.

Third, nobody really understood what "technology transfer"

meant. It was not a simple matter of taking a concept or device developed in a federal laboratory, slapping a label on it and selling it to an eager public. The process would prove to be long, expensive, risky and subject to a particularly brutal form of Murphy's Law (whatever can go wrong, will go wrong). Dave and his partners would be wizened and bloodied before they commercialized their first product. That's why Dave prefers the term "technology commercialization" to "tech transfer."

"We were ahead of the times by five or six years," said Jim.

Congress, with New Mexico Senators Pete Domenici and Jeff Bingaman in the forefront, beefed up the 1986 law with the National Competitiveness Technology Transfer Act of 1989, introduced during a period of uneasiness over defense spending cuts announced by then Defense Secretary Dick Cheney. It included the weapons labs and allowed all labs to enter into Cooperative Research and Development Agreements (CRADAs) with universities and private industry. It also protected new technologies with patents or copyrights and gave Sandia and Los Alamos a technology transfer mission. But the CRADAs, because of their cost, were primarily used by big companies.

"The 1989 legislation had teeth. Still, it was a real slog," said Dave. "It was a decade of slogging. It was very frustrating."

The Department of Energy established the Albuquerque Liaison Office (ALO), with Vic Berniclau in charge of interpreting the 1989 act and writing white papers, aided by Ray Radosevich, then on sabbatical from UNM. "The ALO was the most important development at the time, but the Washington lawyers took the guts out of the white papers. Still, Vic made a very positive contribution," Ray said.

In 1990 Sen. Jeff Bingaman organized a Tech Transfer Advisory Committee and invited Dave to join. It was the first such group in the state. They explored the issues, talked about how to change lab culture and policy, and wrote federal legislation. Dave and Jim helped draft the National Laboratories Partnership Improvement Act, which provided funding to support technology commercialization, required the labs to establish small-business advocacy and assistance programs, and created a tech-transfer coordinator. It forced the labs to take tech transfer seriously. Suddenly, there were federally funded programs to promote commercialization of previously classified technology. The act also authorized Sandia's Technology Licensing Program.

"Once the labs got involved, we thought things would change," said Chuck Wellborn. "We thought things were going to be busting out all over, but it didn't turn out that way. Because everyone expected the labs to make things happen, local government and industry support of technology commercialization seemed unnecessary. It turned out that the labs were talking the talk primarily because they felt pressure from the senators. The labs, to survive, need a reason for Congress to give them $50 million here, $50 million there. Tech transfer was not going to bring in the resources they needed."

The labs did eventually throw a substantial amount of money at tech transfer, Chuck said, "but they seldom hired the kinds of people who knew how to do it, and the labs lacked the will to make it a reality. It's really difficult to do tech transfer. Venture capitalists are a tough crowd to please, and if you tell them they have to jump through all kinds of hoops just to talk to a researcher, they're gone.

"There were a lot of executive orders and legislation directing the agencies to participate, and initially the DOE said, 'It doesn't apply to us.' That's why Domenici and Bingaman wrote the laws. The DOE was marching to its own tune without much scrutiny, and it carried over into tech transfer. The legislation was an attempt to get them in line."

Tech Transfer Act of 1989

In July 1989 both Sen. Pete Domenici and Sen. Jeff Bingaman spoke on the Senate floor about the National Defense Energy Technology Transfer Act of 1989.

Domenici said: "When I first started working on this legislation, some described doing business with the Department of Energy as slow, tedious, uncertain, and unrewarding. Some had the view that the weapons laboratories were still secretive, walled-off enclaves and should remain that way. The prevailing view outside DOE was that technology transfer wasn't working at the department. It was taking an average of 18 months to process a routine patent waiver. In some instances the delay was as long as 52 months. One reason cited by GAO was that technology transfer was given a very low priority among the work that the patent lawyers were assigned. A company wanting to do cooperative research with one of the national laboratories had to negotiate at least nine different agreements—more than 4 inches worth of documents. DOE felt that it was exempt from the Executive Order under which the President called for all federal agencies to make technology transfer a top priority.

"But that was then, and now is now, and now is better. With this new law, the future can be even better."

Bingaman pointed out that tech transfer would now be a mission of the labs—even the defense labs.

"Certainly, the (defense) laboratories have demonstrated successes in technology transfer into the private sector... But officials at Los Alamos and Sandia would agree that the effectiveness of this effort can be significantly enhanced if: First, industry is made more aware of... laboratory research and development capabilities and activities; second, commercialization of technologies developed in connection with the...laboratories' research... through technology transfer is established as a significant element of the mission; third, the (defense) laboratories are made more aware of industry market requirements; and fourth, industry becomes more involved with the activities of laboratories at an early enough time in the research and development process to provide guidance on the development of commercially viable products."

The National Defense Energy Technology Transfer Act of 1989 approached these objectives in several ways, Bingaman said. First, it made technology transfer and commercialization a specified mission of our national laboratories. Second, it established a framework for the DOE defense labs' entrance into cooperative research and development agreements with universities, industry, and other third parties. And third, it clarified and streamlined the transfer of certain rights in inventions and computer software. He emphasized that improving the labs' tech transfer mission were "complementary to and supportive of the laboratories' national security mission."

7

Walking the Walk

While others continued to talk about technology transfer, Quatro was acting. "For the first year, Jim and George scoured universities, labs and other places for commercialization opportunities," Dave said. "They looked at 105 opportunities in about nine months—all kinds of wild stuff—and concluded that none were worth a damn.

"It was very exploratory in New Mexico and across the nation. In New Mexico we had a couple-year lead on the rest of the world. We thought we'd find great technology and convert it to products. We found there were a lot of people trying to understand tech transfer."

As the partners continued searching for marketable technology, they needed to keep Quatro afloat, so they became tech-transfer consultants to both Sandia and Los Alamos—federal legislation had prodded the labs into creating tech-transfer offices—as well as several major companies.

Dave joined Quatro fulltime in March 1990 and wore two hats for the next year as Quatro vice president and paid consultant to Booz Allen. His hand-picked successors at Booz Allen slowly lost interest in the New Mexico market; it was much easier to do business in other centers of government spending. Bailey left Quatro, and in 1991 the partners added Cecil Powell, a retired Air Force major general and distinguished test pilot with 30 years' experience in Department of Defense system design and acquisition.

"He was kind of a hero," Jim said. "In the Air Force he had been a test pilot and was involved in developing planes. He'd flown many combat missions in Vietnam and was a member of Gathering of Eagles. Bright guy. He had integrity. I thought he could be helpful in consulting."

Quatro now boasted a management team with an impressive slate of experience and skills.

"We wanted complementary skills and market knowledge," Dave said. "We looked at needs and mapped a talent pool. George was knowledgeable in alternative energy and laser technology. Jim and I knew electronics. Cecil knew systems and technologies and had been project manager for the Stealth Bomber. He knew where interesting technology might reside. It was an interesting bunch of people.

"We started selling business and engineering consulting, which we had all done before. It's not what we set out to do, but it paid the bills. Consulting also gained us exposure to what was there. But I didn't want consulting to be an end goal. Quatro was still out there beating the bushes. People heard about us and started bringing in ideas. We were the only game in town."

The first promising technology that came their way had a BDM tie. Phil Reinig had started Los Alamos Technical Associates (LATA) with help from BDM, which retained some ownership for a short time.

"We had known him for years," Dave said. "He came across a technology for water purification when we were starting Quatro and had developed it with Army funding. He hired us to evaluate the commercial prospects. LATA may have been Quatro's first customer. We didn't know anything about water purification and turned it down. LATA subsequently commercialized this technology through a spinoff company called MIOX. It was the right decision for us. We didn't bring much value to the deal."

Financed by LATA, Reinig and Los Alamos National Bank, MIOX struggled for years to find a market before attracting venture capital and enjoying some successes in recent years. Quatro's decision to pass was appropriate, Dave said. Quatro was a startup itself; it probably wouldn't have survived such an undertaking.

They continued the search.

Quatrosonics

In 1989 George Rhodes identified the first technology that appeared to be a viable candidate for commercialization by Quatro.

Resonant ultrasound spectroscopy (RUS), developed at Los Alamos, could test a part for quality without damaging it. The technology involved vibrating the part, measuring the resonant frequencies, and evaluating data quickly to determine if the part was defective. RUS could be used on everything from ball bearings to bridges.

The testing of manufactured metal parts to determine their structural integrity is difficult to do without breaking the part. The field of nondestructive testing has been around a long time, but the existing techniques—x-ray, dye penetrant and Magnaflux—could find some surface defects, and x-ray could spot some internal defects, but they didn't identify all defects or validate structural integrity. RUS was so revolutionary, it was selected by R&D Magazine as one of the top 100 U.S. inventions in 1990. It had the potential to find defects and even reveal material properties with a potential for failures that other techniques would miss.

"We began the long road of evaluation and working with Los Alamos," Dave said. "The process took three years. We prepared numerous business plans and briefings, but the lab's rules, policies and tech transfer czars kept changing. We finally received a license in 1992."

That year Quatro gained a fifth partner in Bob Nath, a mechanical engineer with more than 30 years' experience in business at Caterpillar and ARCO Solar. He had also been Assistant Secretary of Commerce under Presidents Carter and Reagan and could speak five languages. Rhodes brought him in to take over the RUS commercialization.

"It turned out that what Los Alamos did was incomplete," Dave said. "Under the leadership of Jim Schwarz and George Rhodes, Quatro got SBIR (federal Small Business Innovation Research) funding and had some early-adopter customers. Quatro improved the technology over a couple of years. We brought in over $1 million in grant funds to develop it. The original patents turned out to have little value. Quatro filed ten new patents after the licensed technology left the lab. We did the early marketing for applications—we tested everything from airplane wheels to automobile engine components."

Quatro still had to transform an immature, if promising, technology into a marketable product. The lab's hand-wired printed circuit board functioned erratically, and it wasn't rugged enough for use in a factory. An Albuquerque Journal story described it as a "cobbled-together electronic device, all solder and splayed wire." It took three design iterations and extensive testing for the device to become reliable and resilient enough for industry. Product development, particularly software development, took another year and $500,000 before the technology was ready for market.

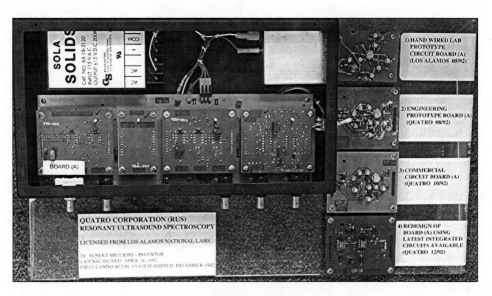

Quatro built a display to demonstrate the RUS technology's evolution from the lab's hand-wired breadboard through several design iterations to the final product, which U.S. Energy Secretary Hazel O'Leary used to explain tech transfer to Congress.

Forbes magazine on April 12, 1993 featured the planned material testing system. Customers began lining up to buy Quatro's NDI-502 to evaluate costly, hard-to-test components used in everything from automobiles to the space shuttle. The company had working versions of the systems in universities on both coasts and was evaluating applications for companies like Martin Marietta, Texas Instruments, TRW and Raytheon. General Motors in 1993 paid about $1.4 million for a system to be used on an engine component production line, still one of the biggest orders in the company's history.

Late in 1993 Quatro created a new division called Quatrosonics around the technology, and Jim, Bob Nath and George Rhodes concentrated their efforts there. Quatrosonics became a subsidiary of Quatro in 1994, sharing resources and a building with other Quatro businesses, but it put pressure on Quatro's financials when sales slowed.

EcoCircuits Inc.

Another promising venture for Quatro was environmentally responsible manufacturing. Today, we're accustomed to think of high-tech as clean industry, but the first companies were anything but. The etching process used to make circuit boards required quantities of harsh chemicals that weren't always safely recycled or destroyed.

In 1990, the Rio Grande Technology Foundation (Riotech), under the leadership of its new president, Bob McPhearson, had shifted its focus from tech transfer to environmentally conscious manufacturing, with the goal of minimizing manufacturing wastes and pollution while preserving jobs. In 1992 Riotech received a $3 million federal grant, and funded five projects chosen from more than 150 proposals. Quatro won a $400,000 contract to design an environmentally conscious printed-wiring-board factory.

Dave and Rich Hoke, who joined Quatro in 1991, led the effort. Working with both Los Alamos and numerous manufacturers, they developed a factory design that would reduce water use by 82 percent, decrease space and labor requirements by 30 percent, and cut waste management costs by 80 percent, while increasing productivity by 160 percent.

"Rich had done a lot of research and knew a lot about printed-circuit-board manufacturing equipment, chemicals, and processes," Dave said. "Our goal was to have nothing leave the building except water, and the quality of the water leaving the plant would be better than the water coming in.

"Rich spent hundreds of hours with producers of everything used to make printed circuit boards. We'd figure out a better way to do things, and would go tell them. It stirred a lot of discussion in the industry and among suppliers. We were mini-crusaders without portfolio. Rich became a national expert on the subject, but we were not of the industry."

After about 18 months and a $1 million investment, including Riotech's funding, they formed a company, EcoCircuits Inc., and wrote a business plan. But after studying the market, they realized they would need about $5 million in outside capital and the profit margins for such a manufacturing operation would be smaller than they initially expected.

"The economics were not compelling, and we already knew that raising money in New Mexico was not possible at that time," Dave said. "We decided not to do it. Instead, we made the information public. We gave speeches. We made it available through Riotech. We probably had a big impact on the industry."

They were awarded a patent for their design but shelved the patent and business plan and focused on Quatro's manufacturing business.

Cable Technology Corporation

As Quatro took on new activities, the business was still evolving. "If we were going to take technologies from the lab to the market, we needed manufacturing capabilities," Dave said. "We started thinking about how to get into manufacturing without spending a fortune."

In 1989 Jim attended a business information exchange between New Mexico's large and small manufacturers. He heard several large manufacturers, including Honeywell, complain about the lack of manufacturing support (suppliers, services and subcontractors) in New Mexico. That year Honeywell Defense Avionics Systems (which had acquired Sperry's New Mexico operation) wanted to hand off production of the wire harnesses and chassis assemblies used in its avionics system products.

"We suggested they spin off their manufacturing capacity and we'd do it for them," Dave said. "We wrote proposals and briefed them. We evolved the concept of how to do it. Honeywell surveyed 13 local suppliers and narrowed the list to three. They selected us in October 1990." Dave and Jim were in Colorado giving a seminar on business development when they found out.

Quatro suddenly needed to gear up for a specialized, wire wrap and harness manufacturing operation. The four partners put up $30,000 each to create a new entity, Cable Technology Corporation. Because of his manufacturing experience—and because nobody else wanted to do it—Dave became CEO. Despite his early disappointment with PDI, he believed a manufacturing arm would serve Quatro's technology commercialization.

"We got the call saying Honeywell had selected us to do manufacturing in October. We had nothing," Dave said. "Between October 1990 and Jan. 14, 1991, we found a building, set up massive interviews—we took over the Honeywell cafeteria—and hired most of the original team. We started with 16 people and hired a manufacturing manager, a friend of George's, from California. We redesigned the building's layout and moved equipment, from smaller devices to semi-automated equipment that weighed tons. We hired more staff. We shipped our first product on January 14. We basically created a new company in 90 days. It was an amazing effort. Everyone was psyched and excited. People did a phenomenal job. We had everyone making arrangements and logistics."

Barbara J. (B.J.) Stufft, one of those early hires, would remember the start-up as her favorite time with the company: "We were very excited to start work and a little nervous. We had a lot of small tasks to take care of and not many supplies, but we worked around them." There were a few people in a huge building, sharing equipment, but when they shipped the first products, "it was a great feeling."

CTC was profitable in about six months and certified as a Honeywell supplier in nine months, Honeywell's second in New Mexico. "At the end of 12 months we shipped $1.9 million worth of products and made a substantial profit," Dave said. And Quatro had preserved a lot of jobs in Albuquerque.

Within a year CTC was assembling about 70 different products from Honeywell kits. At Honeywell's request, CTC took on turn-key responsibility for building wire products, which meant being responsible for all aspects of material acquisition and manufacturing while maintaining Honeywell's quality criteria and schedules. Quatro became the largest New Mexico supplier to Honeywell Defense Avionics.

CTC could move electronic mountains because of its unique organization. It had no middle managers. Technical and manufacturing teams were empowered to make decisions. Customers were considered partners, and directly shared the benefits of productivity improvements.

"For the first few years, everyone was having such a blast," Dave said. "Quatro was one of the first companies in New Mexico to use the term 'associate' instead of 'employee.' The idea was to make them feel more a member of the organization. Some companies use the term and don't treat people any differently. An associate has more of a say in decisions.

"Teams were structured around areas of expertise. The team concept was still new and experimental. The key is the team has to be autonomous and accountable. You can't just call them a team without authority and support."

Team members were given complete business information; they scheduled team activities, handled every personnel issue from hiring and training to firing, determined team and individual bonuses, and managed a continuous process-improvement program. Bonuses were offered for quality and productivity improvements, with a bonus pool based on the company's overall performance. Bonuses were divided among the teams based on a formula that measured each team's performance against its own performance for the previous quarter. In 1992 the average team member received about six weeks' pay in bonuses.

The teams were so effective that in the first year, employees earned 15 to 25 percent more than in their previous positions, the benefits package was comparable to that of larger companies, CTC made a pretax profit of $260,000 on sales of $1.9 million, and it rebated $460,000 to Honeywell.

In 1992 CTC won the U.S. Senate Productivity Award for creative use of self-directed manufacturing teams. In accepting the award, team member Buddy Underwood said:

"At CTC, empowerment means having the faith in people's abilities to do a job and giving them the authority to make the necessary decisions to accomplish that job . . .

"The associates of CTC really do run the company. Teams were set up because we believed that as teams we could run the business with greater productivity. The associates know what is expected of them, and they do it. Management's role is seen as an informational and experiential resource for the teams, not as directors. Teams are provided with all the information they want and need to evaluate, correct and improve their productivity."

"If we have a secret, it's simply this: Everyone from the top to the bottom at CTC feels, believes and acts as if the success of the entire company depends on them individually. Maybe another way of saying it is, by empowering others to reach the top, you can't help but get there yourself. . . . High quality is not costly. Low quality is. Having high quality standards has reduced the defects to 1 in every 500 hand operations."

CTC's 55 employees had an old, 200-pound church bell that they painted gold. They rang the bell when a unit passed a test with no defects or there were no inspection defects. They heard the bell ring quite often. When he learned they had won the Senate award, Underwood rang the bell so hard he chipped it.

Dave articulated Quatro's operating philosophy in this statement, which was circulated to employees:

"Quatro, its employees, and contractors, operate under the principles of respect for the individual and integrity in all relationships. The recognition and acceptance of diverse populations is essential to our success. We strive for full utilization of the talent and capabilities of our workforce and customers. The values of our spirit are enthusiasm, innovation, responsibility, and commitment to customers, partners, suppliers and community. Our communications are open, honest and trusting. We recognize teamwork as the key to our success while empowering each individual to fulfill their potential. Quality will always be valued over quantity as we measure ourselves against world-class standards."

Inside Guy and Outside Guy

By the end of 1992 CTC was building about 100 Honeywell products. Rich Hoke was effectively expanding the business within Honeywell. He had worked for Sperry Flight Systems in Phoenix in marketing, contracts and manufacturing; when Honeywell acquired Sperry, many of Rich's associates remained and were now senior managers. "I leveraged relationships I had," he said. Rich was also diversifying the business by bringing in private industry customers.

Management was becoming a handful for Dave, who still wanted to focus on technology commercialization.

"It was a different kind of business than Booz Allen or BDM. We had different people with different needs. The esprit de corps was phenomenal. Then as we grew and brought in more people and new customers, it created a new set of challenges. We got more into normal operations—personnel issues, turnover, recruiting, training.

"At the end of 1992 we merged CTC into Quatro as the manufacturing division. We hired a senior manufacturing manager from Honeywell, Todd Fowler, who reported to Jim Schwarz. It was a dramatic change. Jim is a centralized, conventional manager with more of a chain-of-command approach, from his BDM experience. I was always irreverent about chain of command. Management went from me to him. I continued in a peripheral role, acquiring business, but I was off doing technology commercialization."

Dave and Jim took up positions they'd had before, both at BDM and Quatro: Jim was the Inside Guy and Dave was the Outside Guy. "Somebody has got to sell the product, and somebody's got to do the calculating and planning," Jim said. "You want a salesman and a manager. Mr. Inside and Mr. Outside. The outside guy is usually a lousy manager, and the inside guy is usually a lousy salesman. Dave is kind of in the middle. He doesn't have that outgoing salesman personality, but he's very determined. I've done some sales but didn't enjoy it."

Rich Hoke moved into business development as vice president of strategic planning. "Rich was instrumental in growing the business," Dave said. "We continued the teams, but they were restructured to focus on different product areas."

Rich recalled: "As we won programs, we brought in a management team to run the operation so Dave and I could focus on strategic development. Dave always considered himself a fisherman. He'd cast the bait into the water, but he wanted somebody else to land the fish and fry the fish."

Sales to Honeywell reached $2.3 million in 1993, but because of declining defense budgets, Quatro's manufacturing division was forced to reduce staff and begin aggressive marketing to attract commercial customers. In 1994 it won ten new customers, and sales topped $5 million. Commercial business, which was 4 percent of revenues in 1993, increased to 27 percent in 1995. CTC had become one of the leading electronics manufacturing service firms in New Mexico.

In this period the empty Durgin nest filled up again when Dave and Eilene gained custody of two grandchildren, Rachel and Jessica, each at age five.

How to Use Teams

If you want to get the full benefit of the team-approach to productivity and not just pursue another business fad, you must have these elements in place:

• Empowerment. Associates have the authority to schedule, determine training needs, hire, discipline, fire and decide bonuses.

• Information. Associates have all the necessary information to make these decisions.

• Elimination of middle management. The management pyramid is flat. Top managers provide information and tools, monitor performance and report results to teams, determine the bonus pool, and set high quality standards.

• Metrics. Each team is measured against its own performance, not that of other teams.

• Transparency. Information about the company's performance is available. During one off-site meeting a year, which is open to all associates, management discusses operating philosophy, marketing, budget and results. Other meetings for key personnel may have specific purposes, such as determining a budget or market approach.

8

Guerilla Venture Capital

Before he left Booz Allen and before starting Quatro, Dave began looking for a vehicle to finance and support technology commercialization. He met the two founders of New Business Associates (NBA), Paul Vosburgh and Bob Rea, and joined them as an investor for several months. In April 1988 he bought out Vosburgh and Rea and their investors, including entrepreneur Gene Watson. Dave recapitalized it with $250,000. Jim supported the move and invested his own money.

Dave intended for NBA to be an investment business that would create a portfolio of limited partnerships. The plan was for Dave to put up $50,000 to $100,000 and three to five major investors to enter at $100,000 to $150,000; smaller investors could get in at $25,000 to $50,000. That would create a pool of $1 million to $2.5 million to invest in new businesses. The portfolio would be equal parts startup companies, second stage-mature companies and commercial spin-offs.

"We wanted to have a fund, but we had no credibility in the financial world," Dave said. "In those days, the chances of raising money in New Mexico were slim to none. I capitalized it at $300,000—$250,000 from me and the rest from Quatro. It was a fair amount of money for seed investing. Nobody else was doing it. But we were not investors—we were engineers who became business guys. It was guerilla venture capital."

Raising money in New Mexico, always difficult, had become all but impossible because of earlier events. In 1983 A. David Silver started New Mexico's first venture capital firm, Santa Fe Private Equity Fund, which was capitalized at $20 million. Silver, the author of three books on venture capital, intended to invest in early-stage, high-tech manufacturing companies in New Mexico and other western states.

He chose New Mexico because Silicon Valley and its East Coast counterparts were growing crowded. "People with ideas are coming here," he said. He described four ingredients necessary to become the next Silicon Valley: research institutions, banks that will make loans to startups, venture capital and "physical amenities." Later, he would say, prophetically, that New Mexico was a great place to live, but lacked mentors.

In the mid-1980s others entered the venture arena, including Meadows Resources, a subsidiary of Public Service Company of New Mexico. The state also had five small business investment corporations (SBICs), privately owned financial institutions licensed by the federal government that leveraged their own capital with loans from the Small Business Administration. Dave met some of these people, including Carol Radosevich, then with Meadows, and John Rice, an expert in business turnarounds, who had an SBIC.

By the late 1980s, the state and the nation were mired in a recession, and the financial community was awash in a wave of bank failures. David Silver had discovered that it was one thing to write about venture capitalists and quite another to be one; his Santa Fe Private Equity Fund foundered in financial losses and lawsuits. Meadows was also swamped by losses.

Still trying to help companies, Ray Radosevich accompanied a few entrepreneurs on pilgrimages to meet venture capitalists. "Charlie Stein at the (Air Force) Weapons Lab had a really good solar panel that could compete with nonrenewable energy. We went to the West Coast and visited a VC. They said, 'We're interested. When you get a local lead investor, we'd like you to come back.' We mentioned Silver. They said, 'Do you have anybody else?' We mentioned Meadows. They said, 'Do you have anybody else?' They could be interested but would say, 'We don't have an office there. We want a local lead investor.'"

In the same period, several high-profile technology companies drew local investments and then failed. "We had some deals everyone was excited about, and they'd crash and burn," attorney Chuck Wellborn said. "We didn't have the entrepreneurial talent to guide them."

In that atmosphere, the state of New Mexico in 1987 launched a new program, which allowed the State Investment Council to invest 2 percent of severance tax permanent funds in venture capital funds with the expectation that they would invest in New Mexico startups. It was soon apparent that the state's money was flowing to startups anywhere but New Mexico. The Legislature tried repeatedly to modify language in the statute to steer money into the state.

The Venture Capital Investment Advisory Committee, which advised the State Investment Council, was packed with bankers who had no experience or appetite for venture investing. Their advisor saw no New Mexico startups worthy of the state's funds. And the group was haunted by David Silver's well publicized difficulties and the equally well publicized startup failures.

"It was a tree they could hide behind," Dave said. "That still comes up."

The bootstrapped NBA became the first surviving New Mexico-based fund organized to invest in New Mexico companies. NBA would later operate under different corporate umbrellas and morph from NBA to Quatro Technologies to Quatro Ventures. Ultimately, it could boast of a profitable portfolio of companies and is still in existence.

Quatro Technologies

In 1993 NBA became part of Quatro through a stock swap and was renamed Quatro Technologies. The partners had debated whether the parent organization would run tech-transfer companies or incubate startups owned by other entrepreneurs. That year, they were doing both. They were running Quatrosonics, and they had the facilities to house and advise other start-ups.

Quatro's business plan in November 1993 mapped out its approach: Identify potential technologies, evaluate technical merit and market potential, obtain intellectual property, develop a financing plan, establish operations initially as a division of Quatro, and spin it out (sell). They would have been surprised to hear that the process for their first company (Quatrosonics) would take 15 years.

In 1993 Quatro evaluated a product for Atlas Wireline Products, a division of Western Atlas in Houston. The pyrotechnic fusing device was assessed for performance, lightening susceptibility and manufacturability. Atlas Wireline retained Quatro to redesign the product and produce prototypes. Quatro's design improved the product's packaging, reduced its cost, eliminated its lightning susceptibility and accelerated the market introduction. Quatro manufactured hundreds of these devices before the market came up with a better way to solve the problem.

The same year Quatro worked with Lovelace Scientific Resources to commercialize the Laser Lancet, a device Lovelace had licensed from a Russian laboratory. The Lancet used a laser to painlessly obtain blood from diabetics for blood sugar level testing. The Russian design was crude and unreliable, so Quatro reverse-engineered the device and produced a prototype in fewer than 45 days. (Ownership of the device was later tangled in disputes among Lovelace, one of its former employees, and Cell Robotics, a publicly held Albuquerque biotech firm. Cell Robotics prevailed but struggled for eight years to manufacture and market its Personal Lasette. It went out of business without turning a profit.)

Muse

In 1994, the partners identified their second interesting commercialization opportunity—the first virtual-reality technology developed at Sandia.

Creve Maples, a Sandia scientist, became concerned that even though computers were getting faster and more powerful, the information they generated was more difficult to comprehend. He saw virtual reality as a more natural way to learn. Instead of bombarding the mind with volumes of linear data, VR fashioned data to resemble the real world.

He developed a virtual reality software shell that provided a flexible and adaptable way of interacting with computers and named his invention MUSE, for Multi-dimensional User-oriented Synthetic Environment. In his virtual craft he could enter and navigate computer space—the inside of a molecule, the structure of the human brain, the behavior of materials under stress, the Solar System. Maples described it as "a whole new paradigm of human-computer interaction."

Maples and fellow Sandian Arlan Andrews developed a companion application for manufacturing, which had drawn attention from industry, government and education. When Arlan saw MUSE in 1993, he told the Sandia Lab News, he knew he had found the enabling technology to create a virtual reality design terminal—something he had envisioned in 1980. He began working out a way to use MUSE in rapid manufacturing applications. Sandia in 1994 established the Virtual Manufacturing and Synthetic Environment Laboratory.

Maples knew of Quatro and sought help through Jim Schwarz, his neighbor. Jim referred Maples to Dave. "Everyone who was exposed to the MUSE technology was blown away and convinced that it was going to be the next trend in the computer industry," Dave said. "Creve's presentations on Muse's potential applications were passionate and exciting.

"I initiated early discussions with Creve to help him spin a company out of Sandia. It turned out that Arlan and Creve, with two different supporting casts, were fighting over who would commercialize the concept. It was pretty ugly. I became a mediator, and, after numerous meetings, got the competing groups in one room and negotiated a partnership agreement. I jokingly called it a peace treaty. MUSE had a shaky launch. If I had known then what I know now, I wouldn't have gotten involved.

"Arlan had already created a Muse business entity and teamed up with Tom Murphy, a retired military officer, who was to serve as CEO. The basic problem was that Creve wanted to be in control, and he didn't appreciate the value of Arlan's team. In the resulting turmoil, they were all jockeying for position rather than evaluating potential markets for their product." Under Dave's peace treaty, Creve was chairman, Murphy was president, Arlan was a vice president and Dave was the executive vice president. "No one was thrilled by the compromise," Dave said.

MuSE Technologies Inc. was founded in October 1995. It obtained an exclusive license from Sandia to develop and market the technology. "The Sandia negotiations were difficult and time consuming because they wanted MuSE to accept a non-exclusive license," Dave said. "This would have been a deal killer with potential investors, and Sandia finally relented."

Quatro provided MuSE with start-up help, business planning and financing assistance in exchange for stock in the company. As executive vice president, Dave was a part-time employee; he was also a board member. On the surface, Dave was proceeding according to plan in helping guide the company.

Behind the scenes, it was a different story. Dave was discovering that talented scientists aren't necessarily good business people. Maples was headstrong, unwilling to delegate and resistant to advice. The problems Dave tried to address in the peace treaty persisted. "He was uncoachable. There was polarization, and the problems between these people continued," Dave said.

The company had a written division of responsibilities, largely ignored by Maples, who sought control of everything from strategic decisions and fundraising to approving the smallest purchase order for office supplies. "He was a brilliant scientist and consultant on the use of MuSE, but he had no interest in developing a structured approach to building the business," Dave said. Seduced by the potential of the technology, Dave didn't expend enough effort to identify and verify viable markets and determine total financing requirements. "Even so, this deal went a long way on its technical merits and Creve's persuasive powers."

Dave helped prepare a private stock placement memorandum and helped Maples negotiate with out-of-state financial people. The company raised about $3 million in seed capital and had some early success with customers such as Goodyear.

In 1997 the MuSE exhibit at Siggraph, the World's Fair of graphics was the talk of the event. Mac Week called MuSE's new software, Continuum, "the most fascinating exhibit at Siggraph." And NASA's Jet Propulsion Laboratory became the first customer. MuSE then had 23 employees and was still losing money.

The company's sales performance didn't match its public hype because there was no product focus with the requisite marketing and sales planning. Continuing management turmoil at MuSE prompted the board to hire experienced outside managers. The new CEO, Curtiz Ganghi, and CFO Brian Clark used their contacts to implement an initial public offering. In November 1998 the company went public, even though it had few sales and no profits. The IPO raised $12 million, of which the company received about $8 million. Dave was astonished by the cost of the IPO. "The only people who made money were the high-powered New York attorneys, the accountants and the underwriter," he said.

MuSE went public at about $8 per share and reached a high of about $14 before the stock price started a steady decline. "MuSE was a beneficiary of the infamous stock market bubble," Dave said. "During normal times, MuSE could not have pulled off an IPO. This was very fortunate for MuSE because there were no alternative sources of capital in New Mexico at the time."

Like most entrepreneurs, Dave thought an IPO was the preferred way to cash out of a company. He didn't realize at the time that successful IPOs involved companies with established sales and profits. "Ethical investment bankers would never consider an early stage, pre-revenue, high-tech company," Dave said. "The pre-bubble stock market was insane, and unscrupulous investment bankers would take any company public for a fee. The Internet Age had created 'momentum' investing, or speculating, in companies with unproven products and no revenues."

Dave severed all connections with the company. He didn't want to be on the board of a publicly held company because of the liability and exposure. The future of the business was now in the hands of outsiders with different priorities than its founders. Dave lacked confidence in MuSE management and knew that he could no longer influence the company's direction.

Early investors, by contract, couldn't sell their stock right away, so Dave had to wait a year before he could sell any of his stock. He sold most at the end of 1999 for about $3 per share and later wished he had sold it all; the share price continued to tumble. "Even at the relatively low price of $3, my return on investment was excellent," he said, $430,000 on an investment of $50,000.

After going public, MuSE acquired a Massachusetts company and a British company, moved to Boston and changed its name. In 1999 Maples stepped down as CEO and later left the company. Curtiz Ganghi, who had been president, resigned in 2000. MuSE filed for bankruptcy court protection in 2002.

"It was a good learning experience," Dave said. "I had been a tech guy. I was excited by the technology and didn't do a good job of evaluating the people. I learned that world-class scientists aren't necessarily good businessmen. I learned how to diagnose business problems and make decisions—it's now called due diligence. I learned first and foremost how to evaluate people. I learned how to do it efficiently so I don't waste my time or their time. I sort of cut my teeth on MuSE. It led to my development as an investor.

"My biggest lesson learned was to carefully and thoroughly evaluate the people first and then evaluate the technology and its market. A thorough background check would have surfaced red flags about the key people at MuSE and their individual motivations and biases, The need for a peace treaty should have been a clue, and I should have run, not walked, to the nearest door. Frankly, I lucked out financially because of the bubble and the outside management's ability to exploit the business environment."

MuSE wasn't a typical investment experience. The company was founded in 1995, went public in 1998, and Dave sold most of his holdings in 1999—four years from investment to exit. The typical timeframe is seven to ten years. During the stock market bubble, software deals with sizzle and Internet applications were going public in droves, making their founders rich in the process. MuSE reaped the benefit of the go-go investing environment of the time.

HealthFirst

A few months after getting involved in MuSE in 1994, the third venture appeared. HealthFirst would prove to be as satisfying an experience as MuSE was frustrating.

Ron McPhee started HealthFirst in 1990, soon after graduating from UNM with a degree in computer engineering. HealthFirst was a health-management systems and software company. The company's products, which assessed and monitored individual and group health and wellness, were used by professionals in the fitness, health-care and education fields. Ron heard about Dave and called. Over lunch, he described the company; Dave agreed to help and, somewhat later, to serve on the board.

Ron was not only coachable—he and Dave formed a lasting friendship.

"I was a technologist starting a business," Ron said. "I had to learn how to be a businessman. Dave also came from engineering and grew up in business. The biggest thing is, technology people focus so much on the technology, they forget that somebody needs to buy it. Unless it's change-the-world technology, marketing and sales will be the toughest part of what they do. The vast majority drastically underestimate the energy and skill that takes, and they're not prepared. We were totally focused on the product. The day we became a business was when we focused on sales, when I got up every day thinking about markets."

Dave was relieved to be dealing with someone who had some understanding of what he did and didn't know. After many strategy discussions, Dave helped Ron write a business plan and then helped raise multiple rounds of seed funding, plus a private stock offering in 1996.

"I was still fairly green," Ron said. "Dave provided quite a bit of insight into how to write the business plan. We had a good strategy—we just needed to articulate it. He helped us crystallize our plan, our product, our go-to-market strategy."

Dave performed an independent assessment of the company's products and the various potential markets for products and helped Ron to establish priorities based on barriers to each market and resources the company had to work with. He tested and proved his philosophy of finding the shortest and cheapest path to financial self-sufficiency. It was an easy sell; Ron already appreciated the value of financial self-sufficiency and value creation. "It's easy to command a good price when you sell a company if you have strong sales and profits," Dave said.

Ron had gotten some early money from angel investors, including former New Mexico Governor Gary Johnson, which helped get the company started, but there were so few angels in the state at the time that Ron twice considered moving the company to California. Dave was the first outside investor, and Quatro became HealthFirst's third largest shareholder after the two founders. Dave and Rich Hoke were both on the board, and Quatro's manufacturing division produced some of the printed-circuit assemblies that went into HealthFirst's products.

"Dave gave us some credibility," Ron said. "He had contacts and set up presentations with people who became investors."

With seed funding, HealthFirst expanded its sales force and

increased its sales more than 30 percent a year over four years while earning a profit.

"The company was growing like crazy," Ron said. "Dave offered a lot of wisdom and guidance during our growth years. We had the normal challenges. One was hiring the right people. He sat in on some of the interviews and provided feedback. In the general operation of the company, money was a constant challenge. The investment climate in New Mexico was always difficult. There were few venture capitalists in the 1990s, and the ones who were there weren't interested in early-stage businesses. Trying to find one or two million was very difficult.

"We had constant cash-flow battles. We were putting together the pieces of the business—customer support, manufacturing—and trying to keep one step ahead of sales. Dave had lived through a lot of those challenges and offered guidance and feedback. We manufactured some of the technology, and he helped us find the right sources. He helped with key people—he introduced us to our controller."

In 1999 the company's products and performance gained the attention of an international fitness equipment company, Polar Electro, of Finland. After initial discussions about a strategic relationship, Polar began to talk about acquiring HealthFirst. Ron led the negotiations, with Dave serving as his business advisor. "Dave was definitely a sounding board during negotiations—absolutely. We had more discussions about the structure of the deal and the timing," Ron said.

"There was an excellent strategic fit between Polar and HealthFirst," Dave said. "Polar wanted to diversify its product offerings and expand in North America. Polar was also very conservative financially and wanted to recover its up-front investment before HealthFirst's shareholders started participating in any earn out." Dave's idea was to pay back Polar's investment over four years so that current HealthFirst shareholders would participate in the earn out earlier. They agreed on revenue targets for the next four years and adopted Dave's earn out formula. It was a fair deal for both sides and Polar acquired HealthFirst.

They consummated the deal in September 2000. Polar Electro acquired HealthFirst. Ron remained as CEO and also became a senior member of the Polar North America management team.

Quatro Ventures owned about 10 percent of HealthFirst's common stock and received an initial return of $264,000 on an investment of $50,000 on the closing of the sale. And from the four-year, revenue-based earn-out program, Quatro Ventures netted an additional $220,000.

"HealthFirst returned nine times our investment," Dave said. "They were successful financially and educationally. I could add a lot of value to the enterprise and learn a lot myself. I learned new things about creating and financing new companies. The importance of working with open-minded, coachable people was driven home. Ron was a strong-minded individual, and he was capable of selecting the advice that worked for him and his company and rejecting what didn't work for him. We had a very open and honest relationship."

"Adding value" would be Dave's mantra in subsequent investments; he didn't invest unless he could bring something to the equation besides money, and that meant advice, experience, knowledge, and contacts.

Master's in Business Reality

Dave's return on the two companies was nearly $900,000. "I never spent a dime of this money," he said. "It was reinvested in later companies. I didn't pay myself anything. The cash flow was so tight, I didn't want to remove money from the pool. A few years after I started it, I began to pay myself a princely $1,000 a month. There was a lot of sweat equity."

In these two deals, Dave learned two valuable lessons. One was, "If I don't get comfortable with people, it won't work. People who know themselves reasonably well and are reasonably accommodating, you can be successful with." The second lesson: "Don't fall in love with the technology. Technology is only about ten percent of technology commercialization. Technology commercialization is all about markets and understanding the barriers to market adoption."

Screening to Startup in Four Steps

Dave and his Quatro colleagues designed process and analysis tools to help them evaluate the business potential of emerging technologies and technology applications. The figure below shows the four-step process to get from idea to market. The venture criteria checklist described in Appendix II is used in each of the first three steps to help decide if it's worth taking the next step.

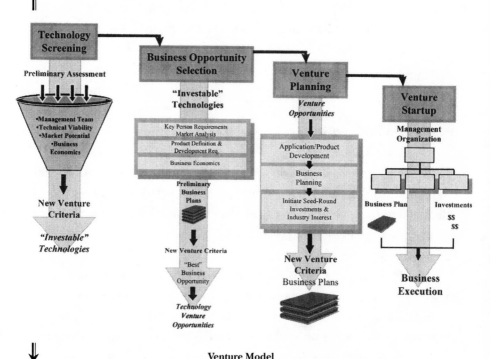

Venture Model

Step 1, Technology Screening, is an initial quick look to determine if the technology does something useful, if there is a market for it, and if there is potential for good financial returns. This step usually eliminates about 90 percent of the ideas as outside of our areas of interest, not feasible, not ready or just plan stupid.

Step 2, Business Opportunity Selection, addresses the same issues as Step 1, only in much more depth. The readiness of the technology, the market for the technology and magnitude of the financial opportunity are all analyzed in more detail. While Step 1 is inexpensive and takes just a few hours, Step 2 is time consuming for the potential investors and entrepreneurs and may require hired experts to perform market research, product evaluation, and financial analysis. Investors will also evaluate the capabilities of the company's entrepreneurial team and assess the need for additional skills and experience. If an opportunity survives this step, the likelihood of an investment is good, and the really hard work begins.

Step 3, Venture Planning, involves preparing a detailed business plan, completing some high-value product development steps, getting the commitment of the entrepreneurial team, and setting up a company. This step requires some outside funding from F3 (friends, family, fools), angels or early stage VCs. The money and time required for this step is different for each opportunity.

Step 4, Venture Startup, is when the entrepreneurs leave their day jobs and when the seed investors decide to take a chance. If the first three steps have been done well, the risks at this point are well understood, but still significant. At the end of this step, the company has enough funding to launch but not sustain operations. This is a very nervous time for the entrepreneurs and early investors because the company cannot survive without the requisite additional investment, and it will not have significant revenues for some time yet. The specific situation at this stage varies widely, depending on the nature of the product and target market. For example, invasive medical products will require tens of millions of dollars and five to seven years to get to market, while a relatively simple industrial product will take a few million dollars and one-to-two years to get to the market.

9

Business Climate

Dave was nurturing his first startups, but it was clear that if the startups and Quatro itself were going to succeed, he would have to become a midwife in the birth of an entrepreneurial business climate in Albuquerque and New Mexico.

"In the late 1980s I was heavily involved in the broader mission of trying to move New Mexico into the twentieth century," he said. "I was spending literally 25 percent of my time working with various other parties trying to get some movement on technology commercialization. You've got to create the environment to make it happen. A few folks were on the bandwagon, but there was no venture capital, few investors, and no infrastructure.

"The question was how to make things happen. The culture of the labs was not entrepreneurial. They were good at what they did. LANL had almost an academic view. There was nothing done to encourage entrepreneurship and a lot done to discourage it."

In 1990, Dave created TEAM New Mexico (Technology Exploitation Access Management), organized to increase economic growth from small, fast-growing New Mexico companies. In a presentation, Dave told the group that the existing business development programs were confusing and lacked private-sector involvement. Government and academia had business assistance programs, but they weren't related or communicating with each other. "Emerging companies need a single source of effective help, not a bureaucratic gauntlet," he said. TEAM was short lived, but the concepts survived.

In the years after, Dave continued his push in a variety of positions for such groups as the New Mexico Manufacturing Productivity Center, and the New Mexico Quality Council, and the Joint Economic Development Initiative (JEDI). JEDI wanted to expand the state's manufacturing base, which at 7 percent of the state's employment was about half that of surrounding states.

Dave found some new allies. Dan Peterson, of Martin Marietta, and Bill Garcia, then state Secretary of Economic Development, recruited Dave into JEDI. "I met Bill Garcia early on, and we became brothers at arms. I was impressed that he was in government, and he had a clue." (That was because Garcia had previously worked in private industry.) And he continued to find common cause with Chuck Wellborn, who Dave considered "one of the thought leaders in the community."

"Dave and I spent a lot of time together," Chuck said. "We'd talk about building a community."

The two wanted to see that the state's support of venture funds lived up to the legislative intent of helping New Mexico companies. In 1990, the Legislature passed a bill directing the State Investment Council to set aside a small percentage of the venture program funds for New Mexico investments. Chuck and others had worked behind the scenes for the change, and Govenor Bruce King appointed Chuck to sit on the advisory committee.

"The votes went from 5-0 to 4-1," Chuck said. "They appointed a bond analyst to staff the advisory committee. Everyone who came in, he'd make it clear they didn't have a chance for funding," Chuck said. "Dave and I talked a lot, strategizing about how to overcome this. The committee members were certain their first priority was to protect public money."

Dave often attended the meetings and spoke. "Chuck was the only guy with any insight into tech companies or deal flow," Dave said. "The environment in Santa Fe—it was clear it was not going to happen.

Nobody else would go out on a limb. They were investing in national venture funds."

In 1990 Gregg Bemis, a Santa Fe investor then organizing Pecos Ventures, made a presentation. "They were turned down summarily," Chuck recalled.

"Bemis represented big traditional financial guys who didn't understand the nature of the problem in New Mexico," Dave said. "All their experience was in more developed places. They were not of the community. What he was trying to do was what a lot of people were trying to do, but he wanted the state to be the first investor. It was a failed strategy. The state by statute can't be first in the game."

In 1993 Dave joined the Governor's Technical Excellence Committee (GTEC).

"There were 25 or 30 people on the list who mostly didn't come to meetings. It was a bunch of government guys—the labs, the university, DOE. Jim Cramer, who started SEA, was also on GTEC. He and I were equally frustrated. You can't have public-private without the private. They did a lot of studies that ended up on the shelf. Everything would invariably come around to: How do we get more government money?"

The Legislature that year passed the Defense Conversion and Technology Act on GTEC's recommendation. It gave the Economic Development Secretary authority to control the influx of federal defense conversion money and steer it toward the private sector to stimulate job creation.

That fall Dave became the first chairman of Industry Network Corp. (INC), a concept that had surfaced in meetings of Sen. Jeff Bingaman's task force, as well as JEDI and GTEC. INC was to be an industry-led, nonprofit corporation to help facilitate tech-based economic development in the state. Bill Garcia and Chuck Wellborn were also involved. Bill Rector was the first CEO.

Dave had also joined the board of Riotech and was editor and publisher of a newsletter, New Mexico Business Watch.

"Sometimes I think that if there were a viable global market for committees, commissions, task forces, advisory groups, working groups, meetings or any other form of group indecision making, New Mexico would be its world leader," he wrote. "This would be particularly true in the technology-based economic development area, where we have prepared no fewer than five 'strategic plans' in less than a decade and partially implemented one. But wait! There seems to be something moving in Santa Fe! After two years of talking about life after defense, the budget cuts everyone knew were coming are almost here, and someone noticed that we are not ready."

Dave also pointed out, in his king-has-no-clothes fashion, that tech transfer to date had not amounted to much.

"New Mexico's national laboratories have a poor track record of spinning off technology-based startup companies. Actually, this conclusion has been validated by academics. Not that it takes a rigorous study to figure out that we have all been hearing the same two or three spinoff company 'success' stories for the last two or three decades," he wrote.

The labs had progressed in making their people and facilities available to industry, but they still grappled with the problem of getting their valuable technology in the hands of entrepreneurs who would use it to create companies, jobs and prosperity

"The legal vehicle that is used to make this happen is called a license, which gives you the right to put your career, security and wealth on the line in the hope that you can survive long enough to make a lot of money," Dave wrote.

Congress and the DOE had made it easier to get technical help from the labs, but they had also multiplied the hurdles. The number of licenses, never large, was actually decreasing. Negotiating had become an adversarial process, "a nightmarish, bureaucratic horse race, and no one seems to know where the finish line is," Dave wrote. Sandia had issued just five licenses at that time to New Mexico entrepreneurs, according to its own newsletter. And even though big companies with big budgets were coping well with Cooperative Research and

Development Agreements, or CRADAs, small companies complained about expensive, time consuming delays and uneven responsiveness.

"Some senators and congressmen seem to think that industry goes to a national laboratory for a technology dole and immediately receives obscene profits at the taxpayer's expense. The reality of the situation is that the national labs provide some good quality bricks, but industry has to build the house," Dave wrote in 1993.

Not only was little technology emerging from the labs but budding entrepreneurs were equally scarce. "The incidence of entrepreneurs leaving the labs to start a company is right up there with the frequency of visits by Haley's Comet," Dave complained in 1994. That year Sandia would introduce its entrepreneurial leave policy, which gave employees two years to commercialize a Sandia technology or work in private industry.

Ray Radosevich that year completed a study in which he tried to identify potential entrepreneurs. He found 213 lab scientists and engineers who had patents but didn't try to commercialize their ideas and 24 who had patents and left to start a company. Ray concluded: "Encouraging federal employee-inventors to become entrepreneurs and leave their world-class labs as well as risk their personal security is an unlikely and difficult task."

"The bottom line was, it wasn't going to happen," Dave said. "Ray came up with the concept of a surrogate entrepreneur—somebody like me connecting with the labs who would transfer the technology without the lab having to do much. If you put the right team together, you just need access to information."

In another study Ray did with Orion Technical Associates of Albuquerque, he found that many good deals were going unfunded, largely because venture capitalists had become too big to make smaller investments in early-stage firms. They described the capital dearth as the "Grand Canyon of seed capital financing" and urged states to respond, especially in the face of fallout from the shrinking defense establishment.

Steps Forward...

The years 1993 and 1994 delivered the first real changes in the state's business climate. In 1993 Martin Marietta (later Lockheed Martin) won the contract to manage Sandia and created Technology Ventures Corporation to facilitate tech transfer. Dan Peterson, who had become one of Dave's friends and fellow travelers, led the effort. Dave, behind the scenes, helped Dan understand the landscape. The proposal called for funding at $1 million a year; constructing a $5.5 million building to house TVC, entrepreneurs and investors; and managing TVC as a not-for-profit intermediary in the tech transfer process. Dan became TVC's first chairman and CEO, and Sherman McCorkle, an adviser to Peterson and a key contributor to Martin Marietta's proposal, became president. TVC began recruiting venture capital firms to the state and helping small companies.

In 1994 TVC held its first New Mexico Equity Capital Symposium, with seven companies making presentations to a small group of investors. The fifteenth annual Equity Capital Symposium in 2008 presented eighteen companies to nearly one hundred investors. TVC contributed to the state's growth in venture capital investments, which during the decade after 1997 was highest in the nation. Nearly every year from its inception, one of Dave's companies was a sponsor, and Dave has been an advisor, personally helping fifteen companies prepare for the symposium.

The same year, UNM created its Science & Technology Corporation (now called STC.UNM) to commercialize technology developed by faculty members, but it got off to a rough start. STC drew mixed support from university administration and enthusiasm from the medical school, which had expanded its mission from training doctors to include research. But it provoked open hostility from the engineering dean and some faculty members, said Chuck Wellborn, who headed STC from 1995 to 2000. Despite obstacles, STC brought in more than $1 million in licensing income during Chuck's tenure and in subsequent years, STC would gain strong champions in Joe Cecchi, engineering dean, and in the UNM administration.

In 1994 Sandia created its Technology Transfer Leave of Absence program, which allowed lab employees time off to pursue tech transfer but retain the option of returning to the lab. Also in 1994 was the launch of Coronado Ventures Forum, a networking event for venture capitalists, angel investors and entrepreneurs. Founders were Larry Icerman, Gene Stark, Los Alamos economic developer Jim Greenwood, and biomed entrepreneur Ross Robinson. Initially, it was difficult to round up even a few inventors or investors. The forum didn't focus on high tech because there wasn't any, Larry recalled later, and investors tended to lie low because if they revealed themselves, they were mobbed.

That year the log jam in the state's venture program was finally broken when Chicago-based ARCH Venture Partners opened a New Mexico office. The state's advisory committee made its first investment—six years into the program. After that more venture funds opened offices.

ARCH and BDM Federal Inc. in August 1994 organized AB Ventures to develop high-tech companies. BDM then had a 35-year track record in technology business development, and ARCH had helped launch 19 companies. Clinton Bybee was managing director of AB Ventures, which had gotten the attention of the Wall Street Journal for successfully forming venture-backed businesses out of universities and federal labs. But BDM didn't really know where to find potential deals, and ARCH decided to go it alone. ARCH subsequently secured an investment from the state.

Los Alamos National Laboratory in 1994 developed a pilot program to work with private industry to identify and commercialize promising technology. The lab would provide the technology and access to key technical capability, and the private sector would provide entrepreneurs and create, nurture and fund startup companies. A team led by Quatro won the proposal. Other team members were AB

Ventures, BDM, and an investment advisory council of several leading venture capitalists. "The weakness in that team was BDM," Dave said. "The company's representative on the team was new to New Mexico and had no credibility here."

The plan could have worked, but the lab redirected most of the funding to other uses. "As always, lab politics played a role," Dave said. "The labs weren't really committed to technology commercialization and LANL went through several leaders in this area."

It wasn't a total loss. The detailed proposal was a good piece of work and became the foundation for Dave's later activities as a venture capitalist.

The mid-1990s would also deliver the first major success story to give heart to entrepreneurs and venture capitalists. In 1995 Robert Bryan and Tom Brennan organized MicroOptical Devices (MODE), transferred technology they developed at Sandia (vertical-cavity surface-emitting lasers), and opened a semiconductor fabrication plant the following year. MODE raised $5.6 million from ARCH Venture Partners, Murphree Venture Partners, and multiple out-of-state funds and private investors. The company was later sold to EMCORE, which expanded the operation and continues to operate in Albuquerque.

...and Backward

Congress in 1995 reversed the progress of technology commercialization. The labs lost funding for tech transfer, and Sandia cut back its program. "Just when some of the Department of Energy labs were starting to take their appropriate place as partners in the local, state and federal economies, the new Republican Congress is crying 'industrial policy' and trying to dismantle all of the country's bipartisan defense conversion programs," Dave wrote.

"Well, I've got news for them—you can't put the tech transfer genie back in the bottle! The federal policies, practices and attitudes that deterred technology transfer from our national labs for half a century have been irreversibly changed for the better. A decade of bipartisan federal legislation has enabled, if not forced, technology transfer and has helped get the government out of the way of high-tech entrepreneurs. As a result, New Mexico's economy will benefit for years to come."

Shifting national politics and federal policies were then de-emphasizing tech transfer as a national lab mission. There was even debate about dismantling the DOE. The labs themselves expected job cuts and restructuring.

"An economic development strategy that includes aggressive technology transfer and thoughtful privatization can produce a right-sized DOE lab system and a robust private-sector economy in regions that are currently dependent on federal budgets for their survival," Dave wrote. He worried aloud that Congress and the DOE would rebuild barriers to technology paid for with taxpayer dollars.

During the 1990s, two attempts at establishing business incubators fell on their swords. The New Mexico Business Innovation Center, a city facility, had opened late in 1985 to support fledgling companies by providing low-cost space, services and management help. It had an impressive roster of business people (including Dave) on its board of directors as well as a number of promising early entrepreneurs. But its director was a city employee with no business experience. Despite good intentions, the incubator never lived up to the models of other cities, and the city pulled the plug in 1992.

In 1997 the Lovelace Respiratory Research Institute, an independent research organization founded in 1947, had excess space. Dave had gotten to know the institute's director, Bob Rubin, and with Chuck Wellborn, who then headed UNM's Science & Technology Corporation, they hatched a plan. The institute and UNM joined to create an incubator, Business Technology Group. By 1998 it had 41 companies. Dave served on the board. BTG, sadly, couldn't get funding from the state. The Legislature was willing but not Govenor Gary Johnson, who vetoed funding.

…and Forward

During the 1990s, Albuquerque added more high-tech companies, such as Sumitomo Sitix Silicon (now called Sumco USA) and Xilinx to others that had arrived in the 1980s—Intel, Honeywell, Philips. Albuquerque had a new image of itself: "Silicon Mesa."

In the late 1990s two trade associations organized to promote tech industries. They were the New Mexico Optics Industry Association, started in 1998 by scientist Art Guenther and entrepreneur Boyd Hunter, and the New Mexico Information Technology & Software Association, started by Randy Burge in 1999, with help from venture capitalist Tom Stephenson, attorney Bonnie Paisley and Chuck Wellborn.

In 2000 leaders from the public and private sectors launched the Next Generation Economy Initiative, a new kind of economic development approach based on support of industry clusters, particularly high tech clusters. The idea was to recruit, retain and build an industry cluster with all the necessary elements—manufacturing, suppliers, educational institutions that trained workers, and support organizations that provided services. Dave and Chuck Wellborn were both heavily involved as co-chairmen of the electronics study committee.

In June the working groups reported. Dave and Chuck said that electronics companies needed a technology commercialization center and a microelectronics manufacturing facility to produce prototypes and manufacture in small quantities. All the clusters needed trained workers, and they all wanted better access to Sandia and UNM.

Next Generation Economy Inc. was organized in 2000. It absorbed Business Technology Group so that NextGen could use BTG's nonprofit shell to become a Community Reuse Organization eligible for federal funding. Mike Skaggs became its CEO. Banker Larry Willard was chairman, and Dave was vice chairman. From the beginning, there was an undercurrent of competition between NextGen and TVC that never abated. NextGen introduced the cluster concept in New Mexico, but the concept didn't take root in the way founders envisioned it.

"There was probably a meeting a day going on," Dave recalled. "There was a lot of talking. Every time a politician said anything, another committee would be formed. I began to ask myself how much time I should spend trying to help and not tend to my own knitting. I had to pull back and sort it out."

If Dave hadn't already made that decision, the demands of his own business would soon force him to step back.

Commercialization

What does it take to successfully commercialize a technology application?

- A technology application that provides a verifiable solution to a market-driven need or opportunity.
- The market insight, access and analytical tools required to assess your competitive position and to demonstrate the preferential position of your product.
- The technical skills and market knowledge required to develop a product that meets the market need or opportunity including performance, regulatory and cost requirements.
- The technical and operational skills and experience required to design the product for efficient manufacturing and to produce it at or below cost targets.
- The marketing and sales expertise and experience to establish and manage the appropriate sales plan and distribution channels.
- The management skills and experience required to successfully plan, fund and implement all of the above.
- The ability to raise and manage the funds to accomplish all of the above.

Technology commercialization is a team sport. No one can do all of these things alone. Alliance negotiating and team building are fundamental to success.

10

Stress Fractures

Quatro's diverse segments performed well through the early 1990s. Sales had multiplied year after year, from $103,401 in 1989 to $7.5 million in 1995. By then, Quatro had 90 employees, mostly in manufacturing.

But defense spending had been declining since about 1985. Honeywell's Defense Avionics Division, which specialized in electronic control systems for aerospace, was restructured, which shrank employment at its Albuquerque plant from 1,900 in 1992 to 1,350 in 1995.

"By the mid-1990s we had a lot going on—consulting, manufacturing, and technology commercialization," Dave said. "We expanded the building and grew infrastructure. All have their challenges. We decided we were incubating companies and moved into a second building, which was designed to function as an incubator. There was a lot of experimentation going on."

Quatro had more than 21,000 square feet of space in two buildings, one at 6100 Jefferson NE, which housed the manufacturing operation, and the second on Balloon Park Road for the other businesses—consulting, Quatrosonics, EcoCircuits and Quatro Technologies. Quatro hosted the first New Mexico Technology Showcase at its incubator; Dave was emcee, and Senators Domenici and Bingaman both participated.

"The partners were still busting their butts to make this work," Dave said. "We had four and then five very strong personalities. We tried to make everyone feel successful at something they wanted to do. It worked for five years. There was always tension. One of our early mistakes was that Quatro's board of directors consisted of the five partners. We didn't really have a board. There were strains, differences in management style—a bunch of issues between the partners."

Jim recalled: "The team was asymmetric. Dave and I had money. The banks only wanted to talk to us. We had broken Quatro into parts. There was no commonality among the parts. We had a team, but somebody's gotta be nominally in charge. It was not my job to manage these senior people day to day. Everybody had specific things they wanted to get out of it. We had different agendas. You need some common purpose, and we didn't have it."

Personal differences were exacerbated by the company's financial situation. Costs to develop the Quatrosonics technology and support Quatro Technologies had turned the bottom line red. This would lead to heavy borrowing, near insolvency and cash-flow problems in the next year. In 1996 Quatro imploded. Jim fired George Rhodes and subsequently quit. After much rancor and the filing of lawsuits, Quatro bought George's stock.

In the tense aftermath, Dave called Jim to say, "Our friendship is more important than all this. You say the word, and we'll give up the whole thing and go do something different," Jim recalled.

Dave said, "I went over to his house and we talked things through. Over a couple of tall cool ones, we put together the seeds of the restructuring."

Rich Hoke, a senior manager who had gotten to know Quatro's principals, observes: "It's difficult to have partners. Sooner or later they will come to a disagreement over the focus of the company because all businesses morph over time. The original intent of the company had changed. They didn't necessarily lose interest in the business, but they refocused their energies on where they had interests. They were all very strong individuals. Board meetings were very entertaining."

"When we started Quatro, we thought we could replicate BDM's synergy," Dave said. "But at BDM, we had the perfect combination. We had complementary skills, clear lines of responsibility, a clear business focus, and social relationships outside of work. It worked well. It helped that we had a strong market. With Quatro, we had no well-defined strategic plan with defined roles and responsibilities. We were making it up as we went along. You need to have a clearly stated vision and a strategic plan. Then you can describe roles and responsibilities and choose appropriate partners."

Splitting the Sheets

Dave became CEO and began a top-to-bottom restructuring. "I wanted to divest Quatro of everything except manufacturing and Quatro Technologies," Dave said. Jim Schwarz and Bob Nath acquired Quatrosonics and renamed it Quasar. Cecil Powell acquired the consulting business, and renamed it Strategic Technologies Inc.; after ten years, he retired. Both companies separated from Quatro and moved to new locations.

The transactions were largely done through stock swaps, which reduced outstanding stock by 40 percent, and the new owners inherited the debt of their business segments. The manufacturing unit became Quatro Products Group, managed by Rich Hoke.

"Those six months were pretty challenging," Dave said. "I was negotiating with Jim and Bob to divest Quasar and with Cecil to sell the consulting business and going through a transition in manufacturing. We also had a lot of debt guaranteed by all of us. Those with the deepest pockets were at the greatest risk. My vulnerability was greater. I didn't have time to be scared. I was too busy trying not to drown.

"The restructuring proved to be a win-win. Everybody came out happy. It allowed us to focus on manufacturing. Business was good except for the cash problem. I was on the hook for everything, but the bank was happy to sink the hook in deeper. I negotiated a deal to buy

George out. It was another hit on cash. We had taken on more debt than we probably should have, but as long as the business was growing, it could service the debt."

Dave became the majority owner of Quatro stock and the only guarantor. He moved quickly to negotiate a larger line of credit, stabilize the remaining Quatro segments, and move everything into the manufacturing building. He prepared a new business plan. Quatro would be a technology company that incubated technology-based products and businesses in exchange for fees and stock. It would provide business services for start-up and development-stage electronic technology companies—technology appraisal and market analysis, product development and manufacturing, business planning, and business formation and operation.

"It was an interesting journey, and it had all occurred in less than seven years," Dave said. "Jim and I were able to maintain the friendship. We took a messy situation and made the best of it."

Quasar had $750,000 in debt, but it became a successful company. With the help of Dave and Ray Radosevich, Quasar later raised $3 million in equity capital from Valley Ventures. In a subsequent financing round in 2005, both Quatro Ventures and Dave personally invested in Quasar. "Quasar was a good investment. We more than doubled our money in less than two years."

Quasar would also spin out two companies, Exagen Diagnostics and Vibrant Corporation, before it was sold in 2007 to Illinois Tool Works. Quasar's nondestructive test systems are used by auto parts manufacturers around the world to test engine and suspension components.

"I have no heartburn with anybody," said Jim. I had a lot of fun with George and Cecil. There's no bitterness. I came out ahead."

Reinventing Quatro

Now flying solo for the first time since his PDI days, Dave faced a host of challenges in 1997. He needed an additional $1 million to

$2 million in operating capital, and he had to make the new strategy work.

His plan for Quatro Technologies included offering entrepreneurs a variety of services, such as consulting, financing (seed financing and help with private placement offerings and initial public offerings), loans (startup loans and help with bank loans). It would assist in mergers, acquisitions and joint ventures, as well as government contracts and grants. It would provide business planning and budgeting, marketing, accounting, human resources. And through its corporate sister, Quatro Products Group, it could manufacture products.

It would, in short, do all those things startup entrepreneurs would do if only they had the expertise and money. Its customers were then HealthFirst and MuSE. Quatro Technologies owned 10 percent of HealthFirst and 5 percent of MuSE.

Quatro Products Group (formerly CTC) was flourishing. The company then had 48 employees producing 136 different products. It had expanded from wire products to printed circuit card assembly, electromechanical assembly, final assembly, product testing and repair, electronic product design development and final-performance testing. It was operating in 11,260 square feet of leased office and manufacturing space.

From its initial contract with Honeywell in 1990, manufacturing sales had risen steadily from $1.9 million in fiscal year 1991 to $8.3 million in fiscal 1997, without external equity capital. The customer base had grown from one company to fifteen.

Dave's plan was working. The Honeywell deal had given Quatro electronics design and manufacturing capability, which could support Quatro's technology commercialization business. Customers of Quatro Products then were Olympus America Inc., Satloc Inc., Devore Aviation Corp., Aquila Technologies Group, MIOX Corp., Essential Communications, Radyne Corp. SICOM, Infinity, Scientific Dimensions Inc. and HealthFirst.

By 1997, Quatro had climbed to net income of nearly $1.4 million from a net loss in 1995 of $52,561.

Board of Directors

Technically and legally a company's board of directors has a fiduciary responsibility to make sure the company is managed properly. It provides oversight and guidance to management, which implies that some or all members are from outside the company. Startups often have only insiders on the board, and as Dave learned in Quatro's early days, it's not a good idea.

In early stage companies, the board has a larger role. Directors not only provide oversight but should have technical and financial expertise and bring capital or access to capital. "They should bring as much value as possible to the success of the company," Dave said.

The optimum number of directors is five, with no more than two insiders (either two founders or officers) and three recruited from outside. Typically, after venture capitalists invest, management has two members, investors have two and together they choose the fifth.

"Directors should bring money plus knowledge of the industry and contacts. A good board can be incredibly powerful and provide close guidance."

11

Dave and Goliath

Quatro Products Group in the mid-1990s was competing against large and small electronics manufacturing services companies, including General Technology Corp. and Sparton Corp. in Albuquerque, and winning about 60 percent of the contracts it pursued, twice the industry average. The company was one of about 20 percent of electronics manufacturing companies to earn an ISO 9002 designation. It was also qualified as a U.S. military products supplier and a U.S. Food and Drug Administration GMP (Good Manufacturing Practice) manufacturer.

The company's success, Dave wrote, was because of its "total-immersion marketing approach, which entails developing an in-depth knowledge of each customer's business and key people. The approach leads to relationship-based sales and long-term customers in a market generally driven by price." He'd taken a page from BDM and Booz Allen.

Dave expected the electronics contract manufacturing market to keep growing because the $10 billion communications, industrial electronics and instrumentation segments were underserved at the time and the overall industry had been growing about 30 percent per year for a decade. He envisioned a national network of specialty electronics manufacturing companies in high-tech centers feeding on the growing outsourcing trend or agreements like Quatro's Honeywell deal. Dave also wanted to replicate the Quatro technology commercialization concept in other cities.

He was negotiating with three companies in Phoenix and planning an outsourcing agreement with Honeywell's Phoenix operation to make a variety of printed circuit-card assemblies. He was also trying to raise $3.5 million through private placement to buy a manufacturing operation in Phoenix. His effort brought in more business, but he couldn't raise money to buy the operation.

"Contract manufacturing was a hot industry, but there was a recession in that period, and raising money was difficult," he said. "VCs weren't interested in manufacturing—they wanted intellectual property and technology. We started pulling in our horns because the Arizona activity didn't pan out."

Besides, Quatro had a new opportunity.

Honeywell II

In 2000 Quatro won a second offload deal, this time with Honeywell's Home and Building Controls Division, which since 1980 had been manufacturing energy-saving systems in Albuquerque for the residential and small commercial markets.

Dave and Rich Hoke, acutely aware of the David-and-Goliath nature of the relationship, spent months negotiating the details of the multi-year, $25 million contract. "We were very sensitive to the potential risks," Dave said. "We did everything prudent managers would do. We made sure that the contract included tightly scheduled minimum product quantities and favorable payment terms so we wouldn't run out of cash."

Quatro was now making about 500 defense and home products for Honeywell. Because of the size of the contract, Dave spun the manufacturing operation off as a separate company, Quatro Systems Inc., owned by himself and the Quatro shareholders. Quatro Systems began conducting business January 1, 2001.

"The end game for Honeywell was to close its plant. We put

together detailed plans. It was a totally new business. One reason we were chosen was because of our success with Honeywell Defense Avionics. We grew to more than 100 people and had dozens of new products we'd never built before. We were in new start-up mode with greater complexities, costs and risks. Our business with Honeywell Home by itself was a $5 million a year operation.

"We needed a bigger building. We moved from an 11,000-square-foot building into a 30,000-square-foot building and invested $1 million to expand capacity. With a five-year contract in hand, we were comfortable reverting from a diversified client base to being a Honeywell-dependent manufacturer.

"We also brought in a new group of people, mostly former Honeywell Home Products employees. Now we had both defense and home products people. During the transition, we leaned heavily on the people who had been with our manufacturing business since we started CTC. Everyone was psyched, but there were massive headaches. We had supply chain problems. The stock room was as big as the original Quatro manufacturing building. We were managing an inventory of more than 8,000 different components. Inventory management was a huge problem. We were doing an early version of Just In Time." (Just-in-time supply management allows a company to order components as needed instead of maintaining a big inventory.)

Good Honeywell and Bad Honeywell

Dave and Rich soon discovered that Honeywell Home was not Honeywell Avionics. The defense division had been a good customer—a great customer—for over a decade. Honeywell Home was its evil twin.

"We started having problems almost immediately," Dave said. "They weren't doing things they said they'd do. They were poorly organized, and in some cases they were even dishonest. We tried hard to make it work and took on hundreds of thousands of dollars of risk on incomplete purchase orders or called-in orders. Quatro Systems would purchase the inventory needed to meet Honeywell's verbal requests for quantities and delivery schedules because they weren't getting the purchase orders to us on a timely basis. When the purchase orders finally reached us, they didn't match Honeywell's verbal requests, and it took a lot of work to reconcile the differences. We were burning up cash, and Honeywell was slow in providing written purchase orders and even slower in paying its bills."

During the first six months of the contract, Honeywell corporate was enduring a difficult, on-again-off-again acquisition by Allied Signal. Honeywell Home began to waver in its decision to shut down its local plant, and then even that debate slipped down the corporate priority list.

"We went from the heights to the pits," Dave said. "The customer was increasingly delaying or cutting back on orders in violation of the contract. Our leadership team wasted months trying to talk to them and work out problems. We ended up with four people whose full-time job was beating on those people to get them to do what they said.

"The senior manager we were dealing with was honorable, but he was forced to retire. They were tightening the screws on all their suppliers. I went up to Minneapolis to try to work it out. It was clear they were going to ignore their contracts. Their attitude was, 'So you have something in writing. What are you going to do about it?'

"We had the perfect storm. Honeywell was being acquired, and there were two false starts in the acquisition, so there was total turmoil. There were new, almost punitive supplier policies enacted before the acquisition. They were going to dump their building operations division, and we were going to be the solution."

Rich saw another dynamic: "Honeywell Defense Avionics still had a lot of Sperry people, along with Sperry's ethics and sense of responsibility." By the time of Honeywell Home, the corporate culture had changed. Honeywell Home had not embraced the old Sperry culture. "When I left Sperry on February 14, 1986, there were 3,000 employees. There are 1,100 today. The product lines decreased. There was a lot of focus on systems integration (versus product development), outsourcing and moving products off-shore.

"Corporate culture absolutely played a major role in the good things that happened with Honeywell in the beginning and the bad things that happened at the end. You could see the change in cultures in their response to calls and emails. I knew a lot of the individuals, and it wasn't the individuals who had changed."

In this turbulent period of time, Dave and Rich tried to keep their team leaders informed. From the beginning, they'd had "all hands" meetings and tried to have managers in place who were communicating all the time. Now they were holding frequent all-hands meetings.

"We started having cash-flow problems," Dave said. "We had stretched ourselves rather thin in taking on more debt. It would have worked if the bad Honeywell had performed. But the fact they didn't was the killer. In 2001 we had a $25 million contract and had negotiated preferential payment, but we had $2.4 million in debt, and I was on the hook for all of it."

Rich recalled: "It was personal. Dave's very loyal. He had signed personal lines of credit, gotten personal bank loans. He was the guarded optimist that everything would work out. It was one of the most stressful periods of time for him. He likes to be in control, and at that point he didn't have control. Dave was caught in a squeeze play. He had suppliers and banks relying on his personal guarantees. Their attitude was, 'I'm Honeywell and they're a little supplier. So sue me.'"

He did. Late that year, Quatro Systems sued Honeywell to recover damages caused by Honeywell's failure to meet its contractual obligations. Quatro Systems' manufacturing sales, expected to reach $9 million, had instead declined to about $5.4 million in 2000.

"That's not my approach to solving anything," Dave said. "This was a life and death situation for the company. It was like we had to sue to get their attention. We had such a strong position, the attorneys agreed to take it on a contingency basis. I'm a fighter. My inclination was to take them on—the attorneys were probably egging me on—but I didn't want to do it if it would cost a million dollars in legal bills.

If I hadn't found these contingency lawyers, I wouldn't have tried. I couldn't finance it myself."

The careful negotiating that laid the cornerstone of the contract now offered some protection. Quatro's staff had carefully documented problems as they occurred, even writing down the remarks of Honeywell's own executives. There was a good paper trail.

Bankruptcy

A few days after the lawsuit was filed, Quatro Systems filed a Chapter 11 bankruptcy petition. Dave was now eyeball to eyeball with Goliath.

"The Chapter 11 gave us some leverage," Dave said. "Once you're in that transparent, legal structure, everything they do is highly visible, so if they're trying to play games, the court would be on our side. The goal was still to resolve the issue. I was trying to continue operating while this got sorted out and keep them from doing things they were inclined to do.

"We put out a press release. I felt we needed some public awareness of what was going on. There were some repercussions from the bankruptcy filing. People who didn't understand Quatro's structure thought the entire organization was falling apart."

Rich said the bankruptcy filing wasn't unexpected: "A lot of people knew what was going on. Materials suppliers thought they would get paid. Employees were devastated, but none of them had ill feelings toward Dave. I'm still friends with many of them, and they acknowledged he did everything he possibly could. The bank knew that one way or another they weren't at risk because Dave would've made good on it. He had a lot of people cheering him on, but they couldn't do anything for him."

Up to that time, Quatro still had a good relationship with Honeywell Avionics, the good Honeywell; that year Quatro received Honeywell Avionics' Ultimate Team award. The lawsuit torpedoed that relationship. "It became Honeywell against us," Dave said. "We couldn't just sue Honeywell Home." They looked at every possible way to salvage the relationship with Honeywell Avionics, but it wasn't possible.

Dave kept his sanity by focusing on his other business. Quatro Ventures was moving forward, and he was getting involved in new companies. "Exciting things were going on. I wasn't spending all day thinking about it. Our attorney, George Moore, understood the process. There were lots of reporting requirements. It kept Honeywell on a short leash, even though they had a cast of a thousand lawyers."

Rich recalled: "Dave didn't let it get to him. He continued to work on things. We'd continue to go to lunch. Dave, through it all, through everything, is one of the most resilient people I know. Even in the darkest days, he still had to get up in the morning and put one foot in front of the other."

Lem Hunter, a Quatro Systems customer, also remembered Dave as levelheaded through the ordeal. Lem was struck by the "high quality people who stuck with Dave," knowing they would soon be without a job.

Two years into the battle, Dave began to weigh his options.

"I'm very certain we would have won, but we were clearly outgunned," he said. "Even if you're right, they can still make your life miserable. It's a question of how you want to live your life. My gut said I wanted to fight, but in talking to people, they said we'd spend ten years in court. There were also pressures from the bank over the $2.4 million commitment. You had a gigantic ax hanging over your head. And there was neat stuff going on at Quatro Ventures. Could I do both?"

Dave decided he didn't want to spend the next decade in court. And he did want to focus on Quatro Ventures. He opted for a settlement.

"It was a pretty complex series of negotiations," Dave said. "Honeywell would buy back the inventory and equipment. Quatro Systems would continue manufacturing, but they were paying us. Then we could generate enough money to pay the bank and most of the creditors. We worked our way out of business. Honeywell wanted to settle too. We still had some things Honeywell needed, and we were able to get some financial benefit. I tried to work through it so Honeywell was not totally burned. We tried to make everybody as whole as possible and then move on.

"I personally lost a half million, and about 100 jobs were lost, although we phased jobs out over a 12 to 18-month period. We helped people find jobs. It could have ended up dramatically worse than it did. The shareholders took the biggest hit, and I was the biggest shareholder."

B. J. Stufft, who had been one of the first hires, wrote to Dave: "I am very proud to say I worked at Quatro and was involved in some way in the start-up. It is a sad day for me to say goodbye, and (I) wish things had turned out so I could stay for another 11 and a-half years."

Looking back, Dave observed: "Failure is an integral part of what you do. One's character is severely tested. You can't ever feel good about the situation, but it was handled with integrity and professionalism. We did the best we could under the circumstances at the time and lived to fight another day."

Manufacturing

After two expensive lessons in manufacturing, Dave was no longer enamored. His experiences with PDI and Quatro Systems were very different, but they both illustrated the risks of being in the manufacturing business. PDI taught him that high-tech product companies should outsource their manufacturing. Quatro Systems taught him that being a contract manufacturer is a tough, competitive business that needs to be managed by proven professionals.

"At the time, manufacturing made sense for Quatro," he said. "But what I did was maximize the cost and risk. Supply chain management has become such a science. Managing the flow of material is a tough business. You have to spend money on the software to do that and the time training people to use it.

"Half the companies I come across today still want to do their own manufacturing. I have since counseled companies on the intelligent use of outsourcing. It's not a natural thing for an entrepreneur, but it can be a matter of life or death. If your focus is to build a product, minimize the amount of manufacturing you do. It's an expensive and unique skill set. You want somebody whose core competency is manufacturing. Outsourcing is also a financing strategy. Your vendors and suppliers are basically financing you."

12

Angel Investor

Through the Honeywell debacle, Quatro Ventures was thriving. By 2000 it was the pioneer in commercializing technology in New Mexico. That year Dave spun Quatro Ventures and Quatro Systems, the manufacturing company, out of Quatro Corporation, and Quatro Corporation suspended operations. With the subsequent demise of Quatro Systems, all that was left for Quatro's original investors was their shares of Quatro Ventures. Dave had personally financed Quatro Ventures, so he wasn't required to give any ownership to the Quatro investors, but he thought it was the right thing to do because they would have a chance to recoup some of their losses.

Despite great odds—and great scar tissue—Quatro Ventures had successes to show and would continue to write success stories. As Dave evolved from engineer, project manager and business executive to angel investor, his learning curve was still on an upward trajectory, but he was improving his grasp of finance. His "learning experiences" were fewer and smaller.

Dave continued to hone his model of mentoring and money. He and his business associates selected entrepreneurs or companies with promising technology-based products from dozens of applicants. Even then, an outside investor would have considered the pool of prospects—what venture capitalists call "deal flow"—quite limited. Fishing in a small pond, Quatro Ventures and/or Dave personally invested money and helped with management, strategy, finance and marketing. He would also draw on his network of contacts.

Each business arrangement was different, depending on the needs of the company—joint ventures, partnerships, investments, and/or fee-based services. Once they were under Dave's wing, he would evaluate and beef up the business plan, brainstorm business strategy, use his manufacturing expertise to improve or outsource production, and employ his personal network to help companies develop alliances, recruit key people and raise money.

The State Investment Council's venture program became somewhat bolder in 1998 under Govenor Gary Johnson and began investing in more funds with New Mexico offices. In 2003, the Legislature and Govenor Bill Richardson gave the SIC authority to make direct co-investments in New Mexico companies, provided there was also an investment from one of the funds. The results have been striking. More venture capital funds opened offices, and from 1998 through 2006 the state, through the New Mexico Private Equity Fund, invested in 38 New Mexico companies that employed more than 1,900 and paid an average salary of $67,295. Some were companies that Dave supported.

Dave continued to work with likeminded people. In 1999 angel investor George Richmond, who had moved to New Mexico the year before, organized New Mexico Private Investors, patterned after the Band of Angels in Silicon Valley. The ten-member group included Dave and Ray Radosevich, who by then had also become an investor. "There's a lot of grey hair and a lot of really valuable experience in this group," said Ray at the time. "It's obvious to many people that there is a dearth of venture capital here."

Said Dave, "Ray was an activist academic who got involved with companies. He put his own money where his mouth was any number of times. That's unique, from an academic standpoint."

The first few meetings drew a half dozen of the usual suspects, Dave recalled. "It ultimately became New Mexico Angels and has evolved into a top-notch professional group."

Dave, through Quatro Ventures, cut his teeth as an investor with MuSE and HealthFirst in the 1990s, and by 2000 had successfully exited from both companies. Quatro Ventures would add nine more companies to its portfolio, and Dave personally invested in five of the same companies. Dave didn't yet think of himself as a venture capitalist. "Quatro Ventures was an angel fund," he said.

Innovasic

Paul Short sought Dave out to brainstorm his company's business strategy. Paul left Honeywell's Defense Avionic Systems Division in 1992 to start Innovasic, an integrated-circuit design company. By 1998 he wanted to use Innovasic's proprietary design tools to clone discontinued integrated circuits and replace them.

The semiconductor industry moves at such a fast clip that products are often discontinued before customers want to replace them with the new products. But users expect the product to last for some time—car manufacturers need parts to be available for decades—only to be told by manufacturers that certain parts have been discontinued. Part obsolescence is a huge problem in almost every industry.

Innovasic could clone complex digital logic devices without violating intellectual property rights. It meant shifting from services to products and required financing. Paul found his way to Technology Ventures Corp., which in turn sent him to Dave.

"We met, and he liked the idea," Paul said. Dave helped Paul prepare his 10-minute pitch for the TVC's Equity Capital Symposium and then agreed to be involved in the company.

Dave "helped me mature as a CEO," Paul said. "I was involved in the minutia of the company and knew every single detail. You can't do that and grow a company. Sooner or later, you have to let go of control and trust your people. After meeting Dave, I was more strategically focused. I was seeing the big picture. I made sure the people under me were talented enough to do the work. He was always pushing me to take a broader, more long-term view."

Innovasic had come up with a market idea and needed help with financing. "The company did a thorough market analysis," Dave said. "There was a $3 billion to $5 billion market for replacement parts. I helped them develop a plan to become a fabless semiconductor company rather than a design services company. Like HealthFirst, Innovasic wanted to create proprietary products so they could enjoy higher profits and recurring revenue."

In 1999 Quatro Ventures became Innovasic's first outside investor, and Dave was the first outside board member. He helped write the business plan and put up $100,000 in seed capital. Dave was so closely involved with the company that he sat in on senior staff meetings and offered suggestions. Dave also helped put together the first venture round in 1999, when Innovasic raised $2.9 million. Sensor Technology Development LLC led the round (a Series A Preferred), and Quatro Ventures put in 10 percent, or $290,000. This was, and still is, the largest single investment made by Quatro Ventures.

"It was my first exposure to how venture capitalists worked," Dave said. "I had always invested in common stock, just like the owners. It was a big bet. I contributed to their success, but I learned a lot. It was one more course in my MBR" (master's in business reality).

Paul entered his own learning curve: "We raised that first round in September 1999, the day I like to say was the day the tech market peaked. At the end of that year, Lucent Technologies was our biggest customer. At the end of the next year, Lucent wasn't a customer. We had two contracts—no cancel, no return—that Lucent hadn't met, and their attitude was, 'So sue us. Get in line.' They were just trying to survive, and we were a small company.

"It wasn't as bad as what happened to Dave with Honeywell. We had some other customers. But we had to figure out what was next and devise a strategy. Dave encouraged us to focus on military and aerospace, which were less volatile. We weren't growing as fast, and we were burning cash. I cut salaries across the board, beginning with mine. I had a drink with Dave and Jim Schwarz. Jim had gone through something similar (at Quasar). The three of us worked it out. I never had to lay anybody off.

"It was crisis du jour back then. When I had a problem, I would go to Dave with it. I didn't always agree, and he's open to that, but usually he's right."

During one difficult period, Innovasic's controller was diagnosed with cancer and was often out for months at a time. Paul was determined to preserve the man's job, even though the temporary replacements he found were often not satisfactory. Dave introduced Paul to a good part-time controller.

In Tipping Point, a popular business book, author Malcolm Gladwell writes about people who act as catalysts for spreading ideas. One of those catalysts is The Connector, who introduces people to others and has extensive networks.

"Dave is not a back slapper, but he's a connector," Paul said. In addition to the controller, Dave also connected Paul with Jan Maples, a human resources professional who became a friend as she introduced Paul to HR policies. Through Dave, Paul also met other entrepreneurs. "If you need something, he gets on the phone. He knows everyone in town. And he's loyal. He's a good guy to have on your side."

Said Dave: "I built a relationship with a group of people I would use as my outside team and would put them into companies. That included Jan Maples, the spouse of MuSE founder, Creve Maples."

Innovasic's revenue growth was strong following the Series A investment in 1999, and management developed a plan to grow the company faster.

In 2004 Valley Ventures III, an Arizona-based fund with an Albuquerque office headed by Ray Radosevich, led the $4.5 million Series B investment round. Dave was a special limited partner of the fund, recruited in 2002 because of his investment track record and his relationship with Ray. "Returns in the venture industry took a beating for five years after the bubble burst in 2001.When they saw my little fund returning 50 to 60 percent annually, it got their attention," Dave said. (Valley Ventures II, a sister fund, had invested in Quasar in 2000 based on background information from Dave and asked him to be a Quasar board member.)

Valley III brought in Grayhawk Venture Partners, Red River Ventures and Sensor Technology Development LLC. Dave helped put together the deal. (Both Valley III and Red River Ventures, based in Dallas, in 2000 received money from New Mexico's State Investment Council under its venture capital program.) By 2007, Innovasic had raised nearly $15 million from outside investors. With this investment the company developed and acquired new products, built an experienced executive team, and expanded its sales organization. After two years of declining revenues as the new team settled in, Innovasic's revenues are growing again.

Dave was now a venture capitalist.

"I never considered myself a venture capitalist. I relate much more to the entrepreneur than to the investor, but I think experience as an entrepreneur enhances your chances of successful investing," he said. "If you've never been involved in a company, you're in for some nasty surprises."

Introbotics

Quatro Ventures' next investment was in Introbotics, which makes robotic testing systems for printed circuit boards. Brian Butler, who had a background in manufacturing automation and processes involving robotic equipment, started the company in Boston around 1997 and moved it to New Mexico in 1999.

Dave met Brian at a networking event at Coaches Sports Grill in Albuquerque. Calling up his printed circuit board experience from PDI and Riotech, Dave helped Brian develop his business strategy and write a business plan. Largely because of Dave's credibility and contacts, Introbotics obtained about $750,000 from several angel investors and Colorado Venture Management. In 2000 Quatro Ventures invested $100,000. The investment vehicle was a note that was convertible to common stock at the end of 2002. This was later converted into preferred stock.

"Talk about bad timing! Introbotics introduced its robotic testing machine just as the electronics industry slumped at the end of the bubble, and PCB makers were looking for ways to cut costs," Dave said. "An industry that had been growing at about 30 percent a year proceeded to shrink almost 40 percent in two years. Introbotics hung on by testing circuit boards for manufacturers with its own device and selling a couple of its robotic systems."

Since then the company has worked on improving and reducing the cost of its robotic technology and developing new devices for high-frequency testing. Introbotics has received two patents.

"To its credit, Introbotics is still alive and even made a small profit in 2005 and 2006, but sales declined in 2007. It's not likely to ever achieve the sales and profits forecast in 2000, but you have to survive to have a chance."

In investor jargon, Introbotics is "the walking dead." This means that the company's value has plummeted from the price paid by the investors but it's technically still in business. If the company ceased operations, the investors could take a tax write off. Most of the investors have probably already written Introbotics down. Venture capitalists don't like to take write-downs, but the failures in an investment portfolio generally occur before the successes, making the value of the portfolio look bad for its first few years of operation.

Elisar Software

Founded in 1999, Elisar Software offered products and services to protect the rights associated with digital media content, prevent theft of online digital content, and permit secure information distribution over the Internet.

In 2000 Quatro Ventures participated in a $2 million Series A investment round and in 2002 participated in a $1.4 million bridge financing round, both led by Murphree Venture Partners, a Houston-based fund. By the time the second round came along, Dave was leery of the deal and reduced his participation significantly from his pro rata share. Elisar shut its doors in 2003.

"They had a pretty compelling story, but there was a ton of competition," Dave said. "These guys were in a niche, trying to figure out how the tail could wag the dog. There were some fundamental bad decisions. I got involved with Elisar because I was impressed by (venture capitalist) Tom Stephenson's knowledge of the market, and I was looking for an investment in the Internet space. Since I wasn't qualified to evaluate this opportunity, I relied on the judgment of others. They were in a very tenuous niche in the software bubble, and the market wasn't understood.

"The CEO was an academic. He was a good guy but had no business savvy. The two founders knew software, but they didn't know anything about running a business. They ultimately brought in an experienced CEO, but they waited too long. By the time they made the change, they had burned through their investment money. Besides having the wrong CEO, they didn't hire an appropriately qualified marketing and sales guy. There were a series of really bad personnel decisions, and they were too slow to react."

Two venture firms and fellow angel George Richmond lost $3.5 million, and Quatro Ventures lost $110,000." Dave declared that this would be his last passive investment.

Venture Investing 101

Startups, the newest high-tech companies, are the highest risk for an investor. For that reason, they're not usually attractive to venture capitalists, who prefer a more established firm. Startups typically obtain their initial financing from the entrepreneurs themselves (savings, credit cards) and "The

Three F's"—family, friends and fools.

Independent investors often follow the Three F's; they're known as angels because they often save the day. Angels are willing to make seed investments in very early-stage businesses, which may still be proving their product concepts, and the investments are smaller than a venture capitalist, or VC, will make. Angels may simply be wealthy people with a tolerance for risk; often, they're successful entrepreneurs willing to seed a kindred soul. Some venture capital firms specialize in early-stage companies.

Seed money is a start-up's first round of capital after the Three F's and may be a convertible loan, preferred stock, or common stock. Common stock gives the investor some ownership in the company; preferred stock takes priority over common stock in payment of dividends or in the event of liquidation. With seed money, a startup can move out of the entrepreneur's garage, write a business plan, develop a prototype and begin early product testing and marketing.

The first round of financing after seed money usually comes from a venture capital firm or syndicate (a group of venture capital firms), in the form of Series A preferred stock, which may be converted into common stock if the company is taken public or sold. This first round may be broken into pieces or "tranches" that require the company to achieve specific milestones in order to get the next tranche. The milestones may include recruiting a key person, completing product development or completing marketing and sales plans. Later rounds are called Series B, Series C and so on.

Between rounds, there may be bridge financing, intended to tide a company over until its next round. Bridge financing is usually short-term convertible debt that automatically converts to the preferred stock of the next round when it closes. The cost of a bridge loan, besides interest, includes a stock price discount at conversion, warrants to purchase additional preferred stock in the future, or both. Often the same VC or syndicate will provide successive rounds of financing, called "follow-on funding."

All rounds of financing follow due diligence, an investigation of the firm and its management team. Due diligence is the homework VCs do to assure themselves a company is worth the risk.

Startups are expected to be careful managers of investors' money. The "burn rate," typically measured by month, is how quickly a company spends its capital infusions.

Both VCs and angels expect a "liquidity event" within five to seven years of the investment, at which time the company is either sold to a larger company or offered to the public through an initial public offering, or IPO. This is when venture investors cash out and, hopefully, realize a return on their investment.

13

Spinoffs and Spinouts

Dave was maturing as an investor and had learned from his mistakes. Quatro Ventures' next investments were with entrepreneurs and companies well familiar to him, beginning with his protégé Rich Hoke.

Digital Traffic Systems

Digital Traffic Systems, founded in 1999, was developing a software-based system to extract traffic information using video analytics, a marriage of computers, software and video cameras to capture and interpret information and warn of traffic backups or security problems. The company's founders had invested about $1 million, and DTS had taken on an additional $1 million in debt.

In 2000, as Quatro Systems' second Honeywell deal was going downhill, Digital Traffic Systems had submitted a business plan to Quatro Ventures. Rich Hoke was providing engineering support, and Dave invested seed capital. Rich joined DTS part-time as a loaned executive, which took some financial pressure off Quatro Systems.

"Honeywell had become all consuming," Rich said. "I came over to DTS but I was still a part owner of Quatro Ventures and still talking to Quatro customers. DTS started subcontracting work to Quatro manufacturing."

Rich became increasingly involved in DTS, first as vice president of systems engineering, then chief operating officer, and finally as CEO and chairman of the board. He realized that the government has a fiduciary responsibility to provide free traffic information to the public, but that meant the average commuter wouldn't need to pay for it. The company's business model, based on selling traffic information, wasn't viable. DTS decided to stick with what it did best—installation, operation and maintenance of all types of traffic-monitoring systems for federal and state agencies. DTS's sales began to grow rapidly, and the company became profitable in 2003. Dave was instrumental in helping DTS forge a relationship with Silicon Valley Bank.

"We rewrote our business plan and went from being a high-tech wannabe to a bona fide services company," Rich told the Albuquerque Journal in 2004.

Under Rich's leadership, the DTS management team was transformed to fit its new strategy. He already had extensive experience in service industries with a firm he founded and with Quatro. He recruited an experienced executive with a background in transportation products, Peter Keene, to be chief operating officer. Rich and Peter are on an equal footing, like partners, but Rich is the outside guy (business development, marketing, sales and investment) and Peter is the inside guy (operations and finance), just as Dave was outside guy to Jim's inside guy at Quatro.

Like Dave, Rich doesn't relish operations, even though he's been successful at it. Rich also brought in Valerie Lind from Quatro Systems to be the controller. DTS contracted with transportation departments in several states, including New Mexico. It had access to a variety of off-the-shelf traffic monitoring devices that can be used for everything from counting traffic through an intersection to monitoring remote stretches of road for accidents.

"Dave would challenge me," Rich said. "Dave can be a real curmudgeon at times. He can be caustic. I think it's the Maine upbringing. He'll challenge, but he'll listen. Dave still lets people make mistakes, but he won't let them hang themselves. I learned patience. I learned to look at things with a more analytical eye."

DTS became one of few companies in New Mexico to grow from a startup to more than $10 million in annual sales in about six years. "As DTS focused on its core market and grew rapidly, its founders left the company or assumed more passive roles even though they still controlled DTS stock. Rich did a masterful job of managing diverse expectations and egos," Dave said.

Rich sold control of the company to a private equity firm on the East Coast in 2007. Dave provided independent review and a sounding board. The deal gave the founders an exit opportunity; other investors could benefit from the growth made possible by new money. Quatro Ventures and Dave are still investors.

"He's been a key ally, somebody I can bounce ideas off of," said Rich. "Sometimes he's the spear carrier to the shareholders." Outside investors own 65 percent of the company and control two board seats; management owns 25 percent and controls two board seats. For the third outside board seat, Dave was chosen unanimously by both shareholders and management.

Exagen Diagnostics

Quasar's founders knew from the beginning that their proprietary software and system had many applications. After exploring markets, they focused on the automotive industry because it was the largest and required parts testing in massive quantities—millions per year. With some success there, Dave began to talk about other applications during board meetings but found little support; the company lacked resources for the market research and experimentation needed to select and launch a new initiative.

"Fortunately, the company's software guru, Cole Harris, was a curious guy, and he entered a bioinformatics problem-solving contest using Quasar's software and won," Dave said.

Quasar's technology, based on data-mining and multi-variant analysis, was used to test materials nondestructively by analyzing subtle changes in the material's resonance response to an electrical stimulus. It could also predict the course of cancer and other diseases by evaluating variations in the complex genetic characteristics from tumors and other tissues.

In 2002 Quasar CEO Jim Schwarz decided to create a new company to pursue this market. Jim, Dave, Ray Radosevich and a few others provided the initial seed capital that year. Dave invested personally and through Quatro Ventures. The company had a couple of names until Cole Harris came up with the name Exagen.

"Simultaneously, Ray and I decided we needed to get Waneta Tuttle to run it," Dave said. "She agreed to do it." Waneta, a research scientist turned entrepreneur, had previously founded three successful biotech companies—Indigo Medical, Patient Technologies, and PhDx Systems.

"Jim Schwarz said, 'We've got this technology we're interested in spinning out.' My job was to figure out what the business was," she said. She was also key in attracting additional seed funding and licensing complementary technology from UNM's Science & Technology Corp. When the company's business plan was ready, she took the deal to venture capitalists.

In 2003 Exagen raised $5.4 million in the first round from Tullis-Dickerson & Co., Spring Capital, and Wasatch Venture Fund. "Now we had professional investors," Dave said. "They restructured the board and brought in some biotech and medical industry heavyweights to create a very, very strong board. We weren't involved in the day-to-day stuff." In 2005 Exagen raised another $7 million from the same venture firms.

In 2005, Tuttle stepped aside as CEO and hired a seasoned biotech executive to replace herself, so she could pursue her next opportunity. The new CEO raised more money, started developing several new products and increased the staff to about 70 people to support his aggressive plan. The preliminary performance of Exagen's products was excellent. They moved into clinical trials with their breast-cancer diagnostic product and created a lot of excitement in their industry.

However, the company was spending money at an alarming rate. The CEO had a $30 million financing deal with a major Wall Street investment bank that was contingent on FDA approval of the first product. The race was on: Would they obtain FDA approval before they ran out of money?

Results of the clinical trials were outstanding, but the FDA wanted a larger sample. This wasn't a bad result, but the company was broke. Exagen's board moved swiftly, terminating the management team and most of the employees. Waneta Tuttle took the reins again as CEO and raised enough money to operate as a leaner and more focused operation.

The lesson? Some of the most successful venture-backed companies in history have survived one or more near-death experiences.

Mechtronic Solutions Inc.

In 2000, when Dave expanded and moved Quatro Systems to meet the manufacturing needs of the second Honeywell contract, his new neighbor was Mechanical Solutions Inc., an engineering consulting company founded eight years earlier by Lem Hunter, a UNM-trained mechanical engineer.

"MSI was a small machine shop with a few engineers," Dave said. "Lem and I hit it off well and began exploring possible joint business opportunities. MSI's mechanical capabilities and Quatro's electronics capabilities were very complimentary."

As Quatro's deal with Honeywell deteriorated, Lem could relate. "What was done to Dave had also been done to me," he said.

Not long before meeting Dave, MSI had signed a big contract with the previous occupant of Quatro's new quarters. After MSI recruited people and bought equipment, the other company reneged. MSI then had idle equipment and new employees with nothing to do. Lem scrambled to keep his company alive. He instructed his small crew to tell callers, "We're doing great. Things are getting better and better all the time." At a low point, he put MSI's continued existence to a vote of its remaining four employees, and they chose to keep going.

"I had taken out a second mortgage and used up my savings," Lem said. "I decided if MSI came back to life, I wanted it to be a real company. I was looking for advice. Dave was perfect in that role."

MSI had no electronic capabilities and relied on Quatro Systems and its people, but Lem could see that Quatro's manufacturing unit was doomed. After Dave liquidated it in 2002, he and Lem created Hunter Products LLC, which acquired some of Quatro Systems' electronic assembly equipment and inventory and hired some of the people. Hunter Products could now design and fabricate electronic and electromechanical systems. They changed the name of Mechanical Solutions Inc. to Mechtronic Solutions Inc. to reflect its electronic capabilities.

"We fanned a couple of contracts back to life," Lem said. "We kept the operations separate to avoid complications (of the bankruptcy). We put together a great offer for the (Quatro Systems) liquidators—we took some equity, a small amount of cash and some assets. It was a better deal for the liquidators than they would have gotten otherwise. I think it helped Dave's pride to know that a part of Quatro Systems would survive as Hunter Products, and I got more of his time and attention."

There was an odd sense of closure for Lem, as well: "I sat in the same building negotiating the downfall of my business and then negotiated the end of Quatro Systems and the beginning of Hunter Products. It was a big loop. That's how you know you're in a small town."

Both Dave and Quatro Ventures invested in Hunter Products, and Dave moved into the MSI building. Hunter Products later merged with MSI, and Dave and Quatro Ventures gained MSI stock.

"He's played an important role ever since as a 40,000-foot observer and advisor," said Lem. "He still sits in on a high percentage of MSI management meetings. He helped me with getting an identity for the company, with getting another perspective on big-picture planning.

We'd sit down and agree on what needed to be done. He'd say, 'What are you going to do and what are you going to have done?' I'd always done everything myself."

Post-Dave, revenues rose an average of 40 percent a year, reaching $4.4 million in 2007. As the company grew, Lem hired and trained a top-notch executive team.

One discussion between the two was whether MSI was better off as a government contractor or with a more diverse customer base. "My argument was that we should stay part government and part commercial to have better diversity. I'm glad now we're not dependent on the government," Lem said.

Focus was another discussion. "He says to focus on a few things and be good at it. My view is, we're too small to give up our kill-it-and-eat-it attitude." So MSI has done a little of both—building on the successes of what it's done and integrating new capabilities a little at a time.

"Dave will back up a decision with his wisdom and his cash if he believes it's the right decision. Once you know him you can structure your arguments so he at least sees the merit in it. There's a long list of people who butted heads with him, and I wouldn't want to be on it. He's a great mentor because he gives advice when he's asked for it—and sometimes when he's not—but he isn't offended if you don't take it. It doesn't keep him from contributing. A lot of people, if you don't take their advice, they stop giving it and go away."

As an investor, Dave's emphasis isn't solely on the bottom line. Early on, when MSI was still recovering and Hunter Products was new, a long-time employee with two kids was diagnosed with cancer.

"I wasn't sure how to support him in a small company," Lem said. "Dave had me talk to Paul Short, who had just been through a similar experience. Our solution was, we stuck with him. When you go to shareholders and say, 'I want to spend money on a dying employee because it's the right thing to do,' a lot of them would say, 'It's terrible, but it's not our problem.' Dave didn't bat an eye. He just said, 'I understand.'

"We said we'd keep him on the payroll even though he was at home. He wanted to come to work. 'I want my kids to see me go to work,' he said. He told us he could work for about two hours a day and then he needed to lie down. He kept a foam pad under his desk. Other employees chipped in to give him paid time off and keep cash flow and benefits going."

The night before the man died, Lem sat on his bed and asked how he was doing. Conjuring up MSI's darkest hours, the man replied, "I'm doing great. Things are getting better and better all the time."

Vibrant Corporation

As MSI thrived and became less dependent on Lem, he began to think about how it would be to start over, knowing what he knew now. "A lot of these conversations happened with Dave," he said.

After doing contract work for years, Lem wanted to produce something he owned—either a business venture or intellectual property. And he no longer was driven to invent something but was more drawn to a new application of existing technology. He and Dave talked about the technology at Quasar, the company of Dave's old friend Jim Schwarz.

"I had grown passionate about Quasar's technology because of my love of aviation," Lem said. After Waneta Tuttle licensed the technology, Lem began lobbying Quasar for a license. "We wore them down over time. We negotiated a license for the aerospace and power generation markets."

In 2006 MSI licensed Quasar's technology with the goal of testing critical aircraft and engine components and such parts as turbine blades, which are grown from crystals of metal and cost thousands of dollars. From MSI's engineering platform and Quasar's technology, a new division was born: Vibrant. MSI incubated Vibrant and began perfecting the technology. Lem undertook an exhaustive marketing study to identify customers.

"I began building a list of names I thought I could sell to—who's going to buy, what will they buy, how will they buy. We scoured pretty hard. I went to every conference where anybody would be and I shanghaied them." He identified decision makers and got meetings. By the end of 2006, Boeing's metal parts division was the first paying customer, and the second, ironically, was Honeywell's Engines and Systems Division. Vibrant also had pilot projects with Williams International and Rolls Royce, both engine builders, and with Delta Airlines.

In 2007 the three owners, Lem, Dave and Lem's cousin Dick Hunter, sold a controlling interest in MSI to its management team while retaining significant ownership. The sale price was fair to all parties and still provided a good return to Dave, at least on paper. They created Vibrant Corporation. Dave and other angel investors put up $1 million in seed funding, and Lem became CEO.

"It was very flattering that four entrepreneurs would invest," said Lem. "At the same time, there's a lot of pressure on me. They're betting on me as an individual. I really want to get a huge return for them."

He's explained to employees that every one of those investment dollars is a dollar of profit earned after weathering the risks of business, making payroll and paying taxes. "It's not like the typical venture capitalist, who would just as soon sell my internal organs on ebay. I tell employees to spend each dollar like it was a $20 bill. Everyone seemed to get that."

Vibrant's plan was to do nondestructive testing in-house and install its hardware and software systems at parts manufacturers and airline maintenance shops. Along with testing parts on assembly lines, the technology could also test high-stress parts then in use, track them and predict when one is about to fail.

"The outlook for Vibrant is excellent, but negotiating actual contracts is a slow and frustrating process," Dave said.

Samba Holdings

In 2004, Quatro Ventures and Dave personally invested $15,000 each in Samba Holdings.

"Samba was one of the few passive investments I've made. Trevor Loy (of Flywheel Ventures) called me. They were looking for new investors. I met with the CEO, the CFO and other O's and after a few hours, I wrote a check. They were in a trough. They needed an investment to survive. Samba was a good investment."

Jarratt Applewhite and Greg Miller founded Samba in 1999 in Albuquerque. The Web-based information provider then provided secure access to auto title information. It evolved into an "infomediary," converting information from arcane government data bases to a format useful to businesses. The company added a product called FleetWatch® that allows employers to track their employees' driving habits and check the records of job applicants. Riding the wave of concern over drunken driving and employer liability, the new service ballooned the customer base. By 2004 it topped the list of firms with revenues under $10 million in the annual Flying 40, a ranking of the state's fastest-growing tech companies.

Samba's sales have taken off since the company brought in a new CEO, obtained additional financing and broke into the California market. "They came close to selling the company once, but wisely decided to stay private and continue to create value," Dave said.

Looking Back

In less than a decade, Dave could look back and see not just the companies he'd started but the companies he'd helped survive and thrive. And he could count three spinouts. "One measure of the maturity of an entrepreneurial economy is when venture-backed companies start spinning off new companies," Dave said. "Quatro Corporation is such a story since it created and spun off Quasar International, which in turn has created and spun off Exagen Diagnostics and Vibrant Corporation. We spun off companies, and we spun off people who created companies."

The Quatro Ventures portfolio totaled $1 million at this writing and is still in existence. As these companies are sold, the proceeds are redistributed to shareholders. There will be no new investments. Dave collected his personal investments as New Tech 1 LLP. It too will go away as the investments are liquidated.

That's because in 2002 Dave found a new home for his energy, interests and entrepreneurial inclinations: A New Mexico-based venture capital firm.

Four Puzzle Pieces

Being a successful high-tech entrepreneur is like putting a puzzle together. The four pieces of the puzzle are the right people, a product or service, a proven market, and the required capital.

Right people: Surround yourself with great people—they're the most important part of your company. You will need a board of directors populated by individuals who bring industry knowledge, connections and capital. They should be smarter than you are. In your employees you will need marketing, sales, engineering, technical and financial expertise. If they also have start-up, growth and exit experience, so much the better. And these people must be able to work together. Creativity is important, but so is the ability to focus and meet schedules. You will need savvy service providers—lawyers, accountants and marketers. Cultivate an informal network of contacts.

Product or service: Many engineers and scientists think they have a unique idea that's worth a fortune. Don't get emotionally invested in your technology or your idea. Do your homework. Study the market. Does your product match what potential customers say they will buy? Make sure your product meets the design and certification requirements of the target market. For example, if your widget will double gas mileage, does it meet all auto industry standards? If it doesn't make business sense, walk away. It's not always easy to do.

Protect your product with an intellectual-property strategy. You will need to understand patents, copyrights, trademarks and trade secrets. Patents are an obvious choice, but it can be costly and difficult to build a strong, defensible patent estate. In some cases patents disclose too much information to competitors and allow them to design around your product. Trade secrets may be enough to keep you ahead of the competition. Getting your IP house in order may be critical to getting financing and will require help from a good patent attorney.

Proven market: You may have an interesting product, but what's the urgency of the problem you're trying to solve? How good are the other solutions? Don't do a self- serving market analysis; get an independent, objective assessment. Much of a company's success rests on clearly identifying customers and understanding what and how they buy, now and in the future. Communicating with your customers will help you tweak your product or service to keep it useful.

Required capital: The seven sources of capital are the Three Fs (friends, family and fools), angels, venture capitalists, government grants or contracts, strategic partners (usually large companies), public equity markets, and banks. Much has been written about the pluses and minuses of each; most entrepreneurs draw from multiple sources.

It's not in your best interest to raise more money than what's needed. Concentrate instead on raising the minimum amount of money necessary to get the business to cash-flow breakeven. Once the business is self-supporting, the entrepreneur is in a better position to negotiate for additional funding to accelerate growth.

14

Verge Fund

As the 1990s ended and a new decade opened, New Mexico's business climate was improving. Venture capitalists had opened offices here, thanks to the State Investment Council's venture capital program, but these field offices tended to be farm clubs for the major teams.

The bigger problem was that money for the newest startups was still nonexistent in the state, and so were mentors and training wheels for new entrepreneurs. In 2002 Dave and Ray Radosevich, who was still with Valley Ventures, began talking about the need for seed and pre-seed capital.

"Venture capitalists don't fund that," Dave said. "That's when entrepreneurs make their really big mistakes. At this stage, mentoring is more important than money. Entrepreneurs don't realize when they're in deep water. You need a lot of credibility so they pay attention to you. Quatro Ventures didn't have sufficiently deep pockets to solve the problem. We needed to do the same thing on a larger scale. We needed a New Mexico-centric fund."

The conversation quickly included Tom Stephenson, general partner of Houston-based Murphree Venture Partners.

"I credit a lot of people with the idea," said Tom, "but Ray was the one who first said, 'We really need to do this,' along with (entrepreneur) Paul Shirley. Dave was the guy with experience and success with startups. If you look at the companies Dave's been involved with, they've done extremely well here in New Mexico. We recognized this was the team we needed."

Dave and Ray wrote a proposal in 2002, with input from Tom and other people. In spring 2003 Dave, Ray and Tom founded Verge Fund, a venture capital firm, and became general partners.

Tom had grown up in Albuquerque and earned his MBA in information management and tech transfer from the University of Texas in Austin. He became director of education and research at the highly regarded Austin Technology Incubator, where he prepared entrepreneurs for raising angel and venture capital, evaluated businesses for entry into the incubator and provided business consulting. He joined Murphree Venture Partners in 1997 to open their New Mexico office.

"When I first came back to New Mexico, Dave was one of those guys you had to know because he was out there doing it," Tom said. "He was breaking ground as an angel investor."

Tom was willing to leave his post with Murphree, then expanding geographically, because Verge gave him the opportunity to focus on New Mexico. "Murphree was taking me away from New Mexico." And he was entrepreneurial enough to want to be a founding member of a venture fund.

Valley Ventures was also supportive. "They thought Verge could be a feeder fund for them," Dave said. "We would find deals and shape them up."

Dave pushed to get successful entrepreneurs involved. As special limited partners, they recruited Ron McPhee, founder of HealthFirst; Bill Bice, founder of ProLaw Software; and Jim Higdon, former CEO of CVI Laser. All three men, like Dave, had grown and successfully sold New Mexico-based companies. They added an advisory board of "other people with battle scars."

Once again, Dave had partners with remarkable backgrounds, but this time the partners all had the same goals.

"The idea was to create a venture capital firm in New Mexico and invest in New Mexico companies," said Tom. "It's a common thread with us. We're very simple characters—we're driven by returns, but every one of the six of us is personally motivated by a desire to do it in New Mexico because we grew up here or have lived here a long time. We have deep roots and ties to New Mexico."

Raising Money

The next step was to raise money. They needed to present an investment history, but had relatively brief backgrounds as individual investors and no track record together. To establish credibility, they relied on results from Quatro Ventures. The offering memorandum called for a minimum investment of $100,000 from individuals and $500,000 from institutions. Tom had been through the process and led in preparing materials.

"We got thrown a curve early on," Tom said. "Verge was always predicated on a significant investment from the State Investment Council. It was the only really deep pocket out there."

A week after the offering memorandum began to circulate, the state fired its investment advisor for lax due diligence. The SIC was ready to invest in a company but ducked after newspaper reports of the founder's questionable track record. Until the state hired a new advisor, it would make no new investments.

"The SBIC ended up being our anchor," said Tom.

In 2000 the Legislature had created the New Mexico Small Business Investment Corp. with funds from the Severance Tax Permanent Fund to plug the state's gaps in investment capital. But the SBIC had never made an investment because the statutory language was confusing. After getting the statute rewritten, the SBIC wrote investment guidelines and began to invest. The SBIC's chairman was Chuck Wellborn, and its executive director was Paul Goblet, a successful banker and investor.

"We wanted to do seed capital, but to do that you need to be able to tell start-up companies how to get going," Chuck said. "That takes somebody like Dave. The out-of-state venture capitalists weren't always sending their best people to staff their New Mexico offices, and they weren't the best mentors for these very early stage companies. Then Verge came along. The SBIC became the first investor because we believed in Dave and Ray and Tom. They had the right skills and could hit the ground running because they knew what everyone was doing in New Mexico.

"What we did with Verge and Flywheel (another venture fund) was to be the first investors. The first investors are always the hardest to get. We invested contingent on them getting more money. Then they could go back to the State Investment Council."

Said Tom: "Raising money is always hard. Raising money for a first fund is harder. Ultimately we achieved results in excess of what I expected."

Tom thought they could raise $10 million. Dave wanted to set the bar at $15 million. Verge I was funded by a combination of 30 people, mostly New Mexico entrepreneurs like themselves, and the state through the State Investment Council and the SBIC.

"The individual investors saw an opportunity and believed the market niche we were targeting was the right one," said Tom. "Dave's background as a successful investor was a critical component. There were several people in the fund because Dave was involved and had his own money in the fund."

The biggest single investor, at $10 million, was the State Investment Council, with funds from the Severance Tax Permanent Fund. Fort Washington Capital Partners, the state's new investment advisor, conducted such a rigorous due diligence that it required references as far back as Dave's employment at Sandia and Tom's stint as a high school teacher before grad school. (Dave wasn't sure any of his superiors from 40 years earlier were even alive.)

"We have now raised $21 million," said Dave. "It's a lot for New Mexico but it's still a small fund. Verge became the first venture fund headquartered in New Mexico that invests only in New Mexico companies."

It was a sea change in the state's business climate and an indication of investors' confidence in Verge and its founders. It was also a dramatic attitude adjustment.

"We have a self-esteem problem in New Mexico: 'We're just New Mexico. We're 48th on every list.' The truth is that we can build and grow companies like everyone else, but we can't use the same strategy as everyone else," said Tom.

Verge Model

The Verge model, like Dave's angel investing, combines close, hands-on mentoring and money in a creative way. A partner would not only sit on a company's board but involve himself in its decision making and operations. The model addresses a second need in New Mexico for seasoned technology business management.

"We're willing to work with early stage companies but not lost causes and wacky ideas," said Dave. "We've kissed enough frogs to get better at picking frogs."

"Dave's got an incredible capacity to cut through the chaff and get to the point," Tom said. "He's blunt and direct, but he's extremely effective. There are a lot of moving parts in a startup. He can quickly hone in on the big issues."

Looking back at the Quatro model of incubating, manufacturing, mentoring and money, Dave concluded that mentoring was the single most important piece. "The difference for me is dramatic. With mentoring and money, you have an 80 percent success rate. Money without mentoring has a 20 percent success rate. In recent years, financial returns from traditional venture capital investments have been dropping even lower. Venture capitalists have become far removed from any involvement in a company. Now they're just another financial services firm, staffed by MBAs with no operations experience."

The model, unusual in 2003, actually hearkens back to the earliest venture capitalists. In Silicon Valley, inexperienced entrepreneurs once stumbled through the business maze, and the successful ones created the venture capital industry. With their newfound wealth, these early VCs started funds and helped mentor and finance the next generation of entrepreneurs. Some of these successful entrepreneurs weren't savvy financiers, so they joined forces with experienced investment bankers or other financial experts. The financial returns of some of the early venture funds were legendary. Soon financial professionals took over this new industry, and it evolved from an entrepreneur-to-entrepreneur relationship into a financial services business run by investment managers and MBAs. The modern venture capital industry is well established in states like California and New York but still embryonic in New Mexico.

"If you live in California, you can assemble a team and don't have to explain a financial model or the need for a marketing plan," said Tom. "Almost all the entrepreneurs we're involved with are first-time entrepreneurs doing a startup."

Part of the Verge screening process involves determining who's amenable to tutoring and mentoring.

"Verge has a lot of horsepower to inject into a company," Dave said. "We help them build a team. If somebody can't work in that environment, they don't get the investment. You have to assess people and be able to delegate, then give them the freedom to operate. We provide oversight until we're sure it'll work. It's a much more intimate model than California, where you open the transom and business plans come flooding in."

The typical entrepreneur seeking venture capital has been in business a few years—just long enough to make mistakes and form some bad habits that may take time to remedy. "The earlier you can find the entrepreneurs, the better, so you can train them," Dave said.

"That's the unique part of Verge," said Ron McPhee. "Each one of the partners is a mentor, providing the exact resources Dave provided me. Knowing how valuable that was, we don't just invest money but provide useful guidance."

Another way Verge departs from the pack is its willingness to work with angel investors. "Venture funds don't often compete, Dave said. "Verge works cooperatively. We'll take deals to other people. There are fairly small segments of operations that align with the strategies of different funds. We're more likely to co-invest with angels. Angels like to get involved because we bring rigor an angel investor can't. Most traditional venture funds don't like to have an angel involved—there's a snobbery that's illogical."

Verge Investment Strategies

Verge's seven-point strategy reflects the partners' beliefs:

1. Invest only at a very early stage—the seed or first round. For a smaller amount of invested capital, the fund can own a much larger share of the company than a mid- or late-stage investor, and the principals will have a much greater impact on the business and its strategy. The fund also makes later-stage investments in existing portfolio companies, as their business models are validated and the risk factors are reduced.

2. Invest only in New Mexico companies.

3. Actively work with portfolio company managers, who may have little experience in starting or running a company. In some cases, the Verge team will serve as management until experienced executives can be recruited. This incubation approach, coupled with the use of an Entrepreneur in Residence, allows a view of operations, so that issues and problems can be addressed early and quickly.

4. Continue to invest in each round of financing, as portfolio companies progress toward a sale or initial public offering.

5. Invest in technology businesses, including life sciences, manufacturing technologies, optics, semiconductors, software, telecommunications and energy—industries the principals know best.

6. Co-invest with other investors known to the principals, including venture capital firms, strategic corporate partners, and angel investors. Share deal flow, due diligence and market knowledge.

7. Help portfolio companies with other sources of financing: bank lines of credit, venture leasing, government loan and grant programs, corporate partner grants, economic development programs, and vendor credits.

Valuation

One of the tricky aspects of working with a venture capitalist, or any outside investor, is determining a company's value at a particular time. If the VC is investing $1 million, what percentage of ownership does that represent?

"You're sitting there, and you have a product that's been through development. How do you value it? Most entrepreneurs have either a weak or no understanding of value creation and capital formation," Dave says.

An important lesson for an entrepreneur is the management of value creation. This process starts with a realistic baseline of the status of the company and its product at the time it seeks financing. The business plan starts with that baseline, identifies specific tasks that need to be performed, and estimates the impact on the company's value of the successful completion of those tasks.

For example, successfully completing product development from an early laboratory demonstration proves you now have something to sell. Value has been created. Validating a market for your product using in-depth market research creates value and reduces the investors' risk.

The more value the company has created before talking to VCs, the better. An entrepreneur should not expect to get a high valuation if he or she is seeking money to prove that the product works and that there is a market for it.

Most early stage companies have a product concept and cursory market analysis. Most haven't even started to prepare intellectual property, such as patents, and yet they think their companies are worth millions. Many companies propose deficit spending for years before producing revenue and still expect a high valuation. Almost no startup or pre-startup company is worth more than $1 or $2 million.

The more progress they have made with F3 (friends, family and fools), government and angel money, the more value they have created.

Ask yourself: How complete is your management team? How close to market ready is your product? Have you developed a sales plan and team? The farther along these tasks are, the less outside financing the company needs and the higher the value they can command. A good mentor is invaluable when it comes to the management of value creation.

The relationship between entrepreneur and investor is one of give and take. It's important to present your company to several potential investors so that you get a range of feedback on the value you perceive. The more competition between potential investors, the better.

15

Portfolio Building

By 2004 Verge had raised $3 million—committed investment would ultimate reach $21 million—and the gears began to shift. It was time to find and close deals. Verge's first opportunity came up before the state had invested.

ZTEC Instruments

ZTEC Instruments designs and manufactures test and measurement products for the defense, aerospace, information technology, and semiconductor industries.

Chris Ziomek, an electrical engineer with a background in linear particle accelerators at both Stanford and Los Alamos, founded the company in 1996 as a design engineering firm. After a few years, he began to think about products. "We knew how to develop instruments— we did it for other people," Chris said. "We thought we should do it for ourselves." His vision was to become a catalogue company, but it proved to be more involved than he expected.

Shifting from a service company to a product company "required reshaping the company and the people and thinking about what we could do with outside investment," Chris said. "It's hard to turn off a business that's successful." Still, he felt the potential for custom engineering was limited in New Mexico because of the talent pool and resources. Companies in that business always seemed to be in a feast-orfamine mode, staffing up for big contracts and then scrambling when the contract ended.

And he was dissatisfied with his own role: "Almost everything funneled through me—design, sales, marketing. Every customer knew me. I was wearing too many hats."

In 2000 Technology Ventures Corporation selected ZTEC to present at the New Mexico Equity Capital Symposium. One of the experts helping entrepreneurs clarify their business plans was Dave.

"We were teamed with a half dozen different people—an attorney, HR, marketing—but the person I connected with best was Dave Durgin," Chris said. "He knew the technology. He had contract manufacturing experience. He knew what we did. We hit it off because of his business acumen and background. I needed someone with more experience and a broader view."

ZTEC presented in 2001 and didn't win any investors, but it did win a mentor.

"We had been a bootstrap company, taking revenues from services and feeding it back into products. We weren't ready for an investment. We didn't have a clear vision of what we wanted to do. We had a niche strategy. I wouldn't invest in it, myself."

But he did. During a period of tight cash flow, Chris told his staff of nine that he was going to take ten percent of his salary in company stock and asked if anyone else wanted to do the same. They all signed up. Dave was impressed.

Based on his own experience, Dave was cool to the idea of an immediate transition to a catalogue business when ZTEC had customers for its engineering services. Chris pushed on with his product company.

"At the time it was a difficult decision to make. One thing about Dave I really appreciate is he doesn't sugarcoat. He says what he thinks. I don't always agree, but his thought process is driven from his experience and his view of the world. He can be brutally honest. He asked a lot of good questions and had more questions along the way."

Dave's questioning forced Chris to think about why he was choosing a certain path. "A lot of business people don't think things through. They're not forced to provide answers. They tend to be opportunistic. He got us to focus, and that really made the difference."

By 2003 ZTEC had a vision and could show progress. Chris made a presentation to Verge and began talking to angel investors through New Mexico Private Investors. Dave made all the introductions to both groups.

Earlier, Dave had joined the board of directors and knew the company well. The Verge partners decided to invest and not wait for the state. They went so far as to develop a fallback plan in the event that the state decided against investing in Verge. In September 2004 Verge invested $500,000, and Dave invested personally and through Quatro Ventures. Verge was the company's first outside investor. Jim Higdon joined ZTEC's board of directors as Verge's representative and was so impressed with the company that he too invested personally.

With the investment, ZTEC accelerated R&D and product development and built a much stronger sales and marketing team, which began driving the company's growth.

In 2007 ZTEC's revenues passed $4 million a year and were racing toward $6 million or $7 million. Average annual revenue has grown by 63 percent. On paper, Verge's investment has nearly tripled.

Dave is still asking good questions. In discussions with the contract manufacturer, larger venture funds and potential acquisition targets or acquiring companies, Dave added credibility and "a sanity check," Chris said.

PatchWork Systems

The second investment, in August 2005, would prove to be the MBR (master's in business reality) for Verge's newer partners. Verge committed $600,000 to PatchWork Systems, an Albuquerque startup founded by a 25-year veteran of information systems at Sandia. She had developed software that manages and automates Oracle's upgrades and patches. After licensing the software from Sandia, she retired and founded a company in 2002. UNM professor and Verge advisor Sul Kassicieh referred her to Verge. Bill Bice became Verge's lead person.

The first tranche of Verge's investment was $75,000 to fund modification of the company's software and additional market research. Subsequent funding required PatchWork to meet product-development and market-research milestones. The company failed to meet its milestones, and after a few stressful years as an entrepreneur, the founder returned to government employment. Most of the initial investment was written off, and the Verge partners moved on.

Altela

The third investment was Altela, founded in 2005 by Ned Godshall, who had founded other companies in the state. Tom Stephenson had gotten to know Ned when Murphree invested in Mesofuel, one of Ned's previous ventures. Altela licensed a proprietary water-purification process developed at Arizona State University. This energy-efficient distillation technology turns extremely saline, brackish water or industrial water into fresh potable water.

Verge made a small, $100,000 investment in August 2005, along with Pennsylvania-based EnerTech Capital, Fort Washington and some angels, and Tom Stephenson joined the board. With the money, Altela transformed its technology into a marketable product and did some research into the handling of water produced by the oil and gas industry in the course of drilling. This became a target market. In 2006 Verge led a $1.2 million round, providing $600,000, which allowed the company to ramp up production, launch marketing and begin deploying systems at customers' locations. One of the investors was Yates Petroleum, a large New Mexico oil production company that tested the device on water extracted during drilling of its own wells. The result was water 20 times more pure than drinking water. The device could save oil companies millions in the costs of hauling away contaminated water.

Like many early stage companies, Altela struggled with its product development and manufacturing and was about a year late getting its initial product to the market. The company's early institutional and angel investors sustained it through this challenging period.

In October 2007 CCS Income Trust, a Canadian energy and environmental firm, invested $5.2 million of the $7.1 million third round; other investors were Verge, EnerTech, Frank Yates, and Fort Washington. Altela's future fortunes will be determined by its products' performance in the hostile environment of oil and gas fields in Colorado and Wyoming.

TruTouch Technologies

In October 2005 Verge invested $750,000 in TruTouch Technologies, leading a $2.4 million investment round that included Flywheel Ventures, New Mexico Community Capital and Fort Washington. The TruTouch technology transmits light into the skin using an optical touch pad; it then analyzes a portion of the light reflected back to measure the amount of alcohol in a person's tissue. The TruTouch method is faster, cleaner and more accurate than Breathalyzers, blood or urine tests.

"I believe that TruTouch's technology will revolutionize society's ability to address and dramatically reduce the loss of life and expense caused by drunk drivers," Dave said at the time. "It is without a doubt a disruptive technology in the alcohol detection market and will, in my opinion, become the detection method of choice within five years."

That deal took a year to complete. Jim McNally, then an executive with InLight Solutions, a New Mexico tech-transfer company, approached Dave in 2004. "I went to people who knew Dave," said Jim. "I did my due diligence before approaching him."

InLight wanted to spin out a company based on a new use for its technology and needed venture capital. "We met multiple times with Dave, considering how to transfer the technology and how to form a company," said Jim. "After an all-day meeting with Dave, we decided to form TruTouch."

The deal was complicated by issues of intellectual property and the relationship between TruTouch and InLight. "We spent lots of money on IP attorneys," Dave said. He advised Jim to establish a separate company, not a division or subsidiary, and to license the technology from InLight. He also encouraged "a singular focus on the market for noninvasive alcohol products. That would capture the interest of Verge, but there were no guarantees," Jim said. They formed TruTouch in 2005.

Mentoring from Dave started at the beginning. "As soon as the term sheet was handed over, he began mentoring," Jim said. Focus was a continuing theme: "It was an unambiguous message: Focus, and have your team focus, on product development. Don't get distracted." Second, position yourself strategically so you can get to early revenues. Don't try for a home-run product right away. "There was a prioritization on getting to market. Pick an early market, focus on that, and have a strategy on what the next market is."

Jim, like others mentored by Dave, appreciated his experience and his direct communication style. "He brings to bear decades of experience in negotiating different kinds of deals. That can't be beat."

TruTouch launched its first product in mid-2007 and found a positive market response. Early users have provided valuable feedback. The original investment syndicate has invested an additional $1.6 million in the company and a third round will likely be necessary to expand the company's sales initiatives.

"Like most start up companies, TruTouch was a little late getting its first product to market, and it wasn't quite ready for that market," Dave said. "Customer feedback and thousands of tests in diverse environments were extremely valuable. The product was quickly improved. TruTouch's first-year sales were disappointing, but the experience resulted in more focus on sales. TruTouch is typical of companies with a strong technical team with no experience in marketing and sales. In this case, all of the company's leaders are receptive to mentoring and they're quick to respond to constructive input."

Wellkeeper

In December 2005 Verge led a first and second round totaling $2.05 million in Wellkeeper, a four-year-old, company that serves independent oil and natural gas well operators. The technology enables oilfield personnel to remotely monitor a well's performance and quickly locate potential problems, which can increase production and avoid spills. This kind of affordable, Internet-based support wasn't previously available to small- and medium-sized independents. Ray and Tom joined the board of directors.

Momentum Builds

In November 2005 Paul Short, who had hired his replacement at Innovasic, was named Verge's Entrepreneur In Residence. This would allow Verge to form companies around promising technologies.

"My job was to find a company to run or create a company," Paul said. "Verge would provide an office, a stipend and access to deal flow. I would work with Dave and the rest of the team. We would look at deals and incubate deals."

In 2006 Entrepreneur Magazine named Verge one of the nation's Top 100 Venture Capital Firms for Entrepreneurs, based on the number of deals completed in 2005 as documented in the "Money Tree Report" by PricewaterhouseCoopers and the National Venture Capital Association.

"Verge's investment activity in 2006 has already exceeded that for 2005, as has New Mexico's in general," Dave said at the time. "We hope to see this growth translate into greater attention for the region, and greater success for our portfolio investments."

Expanding Portfolio

During 2006 Verge funded three more companies.

Verge invested $750,000 in Vertical Power, founded in 2006 by former employees of Eclipse Aviation, Boeing and Honeywell who wanted to build a new generation of flight control systems for the general aviation market. The company's VP-200, aimed at the experimental and light sport aircraft market, uses microprocessors and solid-state switches to provide advanced electrical system features, simplified aircraft wiring, and the ability to eliminate dozens of modules, breakers and switches typically found in modern aircraft. The company launched its first products at the prestigious Oshkosh air show in 2007. "The product had a few design setbacks but is selling, and the company's outlook is good," Dave said. Bill Bice is on the board.

Two more new portfolio companies were founded by Verge partners.

BoomTime, an Albuquerque company co-founded in 2005 by Verge partner Bill Bice, along with Ben Morin, provides instant, printable gift certificates for service businesses. Its first product was SpaBoom, which sells gift certificates for massages, nail treatments and other services from some 1,500 spas and salons nationwide. The model gives service businesses a way to use the Internet to maintain relationships with customers. Verge invested $700,000, its seventh investment, and Ron McPhee joined the board. At this writing, the company has signed up nearly 2,000 spas.

Quadric is a semiconductor company started by Entrepreneur In Residence Paul Short to develop a programmable logic architecture that could revolutionize certain application-specific integrated circuits. It's a company Verge built around a technology and an opportunity. Verge provided a bridge loan of $55,000 to validate the concept and then invested in three rounds of financing totaling some $355,000. Seed money allowed Paul to develop the technology and understand the market, but Quadric is what venture capitalists call a home-run type deal; it will take $40 million to commercialize, which means finding a bigger fund or an institutional investor, which New Mexico still lacks. Dave and Tom sit on the board.

The pace accelerated in 2007, as Verge invested in six more companies.

In March Massachusetts-based Village Ventures led a $1.1 million seed investment in IntelliCyt (formerly Sage Sciences), an Albuquerque biotech company. Verge and several angel investors participated. IntelliCyt is commercializing a hardware-software system developed at UNM's Health Sciences Center that dramatically increases the throughput of flow cytometers. (Cytometers, which analyze cells at a molecular level, are used to develop new drugs and diagnose diseases.) With the addition of super-computing and informatics, the devices can quickly process vast amounts of information or focus on individual cells for detailed study and comparison. The UNM technology can speed drug discovery and reduce the costs of drug development and clinical diagnosis. Ray is an official observer at board meetings.

In August, Verge led a $1.1 million Series A funding round for Altaview Technologies, an Albuquerque company founded in 2007 by Verge partner Ron McPhee, Alan Antin and Daniel Coughlin. Altaview has developed systems with embedded sensors to detect an athlete's heart rate and environmental conditions and transmit that information to a television system for real-time use in sports telecasts. The initial application is monitoring and broadcasting of drag and stock-car racers' heart rates. Planned applications include the measurement of impact levels in contact sports. Ron McPhee and Tom Stephenson sit on the board.

The year's third investment was Nanocrystal, started by Petros Varangis, who co-founded Zia Laser, and former Sandian Lei Zhang, who previously worked for Emcore. NanoCrystal is commercializing Gallium Nitride (GaN) production technology from UNM for the manufacture of materials used in such devices as Light Emitting Diodes (LEDs), Laser Diodes (LDs), and high-frequency transistors. The product is aimed at the wafer market for illumination, optical storage, bio-sensing, and electronics for harsh environments.

The next company was Verge partner Ron McPhee's second company, Nuvita, which provides a health-care program intended to avoid such lifestyle ailments as heart disease, diabetes and obesity. For people who know they need to make changes in their lives but aren't inclined to join a gym, Nuvita offers a flexible program delivered at the workplace or other locations and can involve family and friends for motivation and encouragement. The company's technology tracks results and also provides a Web site. Bill Bice sits on the board.

In late 2007 Avasca Medical joined the Verge portfolio. Avasca, founded the same year by Verge advisory board member Bob Curtis and Wilmer Sibbitt, was developing better, safer arteriotomy closure systems for use in such procedures as angioplasty and stents. Sibbitts, a professor of internal medicine, rheumatology and neurology at the UNM Health Sciences Center, had developed the technology with his brother Randy, a radiologist and UNM Medical School graduate. The two were also co-founders of an earlier company that successfully commercialized technology they developed. Ray sits on the Avasca board.

The final investment of 2007 was Noribachi, organized by successful Silicon Valley entrepreneur Farzad Dibachi and retired Intel executive Bruce Leising. Noribachi will use innovative photovoltaic solar-cell material to produce appliances, such as exterior residential lights, with the solar collecting material integrated into the design. In the company's first year of operations, it completed the design of several products and began producing revenue from consulting on the use of their technology.

In 2007, Verge partners Ron McPhee and Bill Bice acquired and renovated the old J.S. Brown Mercantile Building in downtown Albuquerque to serve as Verge headquarters and an incubator for portfolio companies.

"A huge problem when I was starting out was getting a place you could afford without having to sign a long lease," said Ron. "We moved four times in four years. It was a huge hassle. Being surrounded by other startups has meant sharing of ideas and resources. We've got one CFO working with three companies in here. We'll nurture them until they need their own building."

Tom added: "There's an energy level that comes from being surrounded by a lot of other startups. It's important in a community where that's not prevalent. There's camaraderie because everyone's in the same boat. When you're walking out to the parking lot at 8 p.m., your car isn't the only one in the lot."

Also in 2007 Verge created a new way to finance early stage companies, the Line of Equity (LOE). It's similar to a bank's line of credit but allows the company to use its stock to obtain cash under pre-negotiated conditions without assuming more debt. ZTEC became the first to use the LOE.

Verge added a fifteenth company to its portfolio in 2008— Vibrant Corp., the company founded by Lem Hunter based on Quasar's nondestructive testing technology.

The partners redirected their energies from finding new investment opportunities to shepherding portfolio companies through the challenges they faced as early-stage companies to become successful operating companies.

At this writing, Verge has completed the first two phases of a venture fund: raising money and finding deals. The fund's success with the first two phases is unprecedented in New Mexico, but the third phase, developing and selling the companies—and the financial return to investors—will determine the fund's ultimate success or failure. This chapter is yet to be written.

"Experience has shown that companies fail faster than they succeed," Dave said. "Most venture funds have a life of about ten years; if a portfolio company fails, it's usually during the third-to-fifth year, while successful companies will be ready to sell in years 7 to 10. Traditional venture funds expect 70 percent of their companies to fail. Because of its hands-on approach, Verge expects at least 70 percent of its companies to succeed. Time will tell."

Dave's Destination

In just a few fast-paced years, Verge had a large portfolio of new companies and an incubator. "The companies are all different, and the deals each evolved over a few months or a couple of years, Dave said. "The process is rigorous and unpredictable."

"People told us we couldn't raise a fund in New Mexico and that we couldn't build a stable of successful companies in New Mexico," said Tom. "We've made 15 investments and have 14 portfolio companies. That's a pretty strong record."

The focus now is less on deals and more on growing and selling the portfolio companies. The partners are now talking about Verge II, a bigger fund on the same model but aimed at the Southwest and not just New Mexico.

Dave, now 70, said, "I think of Verge I as the culmination of my journey. In my view, Verge was the natural progression from my early struggles with PDI, through big-company entrepreneurial activities (BDM and Booz Allen), back to early-stage high-tech activities with Quatro and evolving to mentoring and investing (NBA, Quatro Technologies, Quatro Ventures, and Valley Ventures)."

Dave's friends and protégés agree. Said Jim Schwarz, "Where he is now is exactly what he wanted to do."

Said Ron McPhee: "Verge will be his legacy. It's exactly what's needed in New Mexico right now."

So You Want to Be an Entrepreneur?

Become an entrepreneur, the self-help books say. Dave, after some gut-wrenching failures, some close shaves and some gratifying successes, would tell you to answer some hard questions first:

1. Why do you want to be an entrepreneur?
2. Do you understand your strengths and weaknesses?
3. How big is the market opportunity?
4. Can you tolerate life on the brink? Can you rise from failure?

Here are the answers:

1. Tired of your day job? Want to be your own boss? Those aren't good enough reasons. Want to solve a problem, change the world, build a legacy, and get rich? Those are reasons. Entrepreneurs are driven by challenge and achievement. An investor wants to hear you say you want to get rich.

2. You might be a great engineer or scientist, but what do you know about running a business? You will need to evaluate markets, prepare a business plan, raise money, develop and lead a management team, grow sales, and interact with your board members and investors. You must have the humility to admit you don't know everything and get help.

3. You may have a better mousetrap, but who, exactly, will buy it? How will they buy? Too many entrepreneurs are seduced by their technology and don't do enough homework on potential markets.

4. You should be prepared to leave your cushy job behind, invest your savings and retirement, and walk through walls to make your company succeed. Most entrepreneurs have made these sacrifices. They have a high tolerance of risk and a philosophical attitude toward failure. Also, investors want to know you've got skin in the game.

If you answered these questions correctly, you just might be an entrepreneur.

Timeline

1961-1965: Sandia National Laboratory

1965-1967: New Mexico State University

1967: Sandia National Laboratory

1968: Dave starts Product Design Inc. (PDI).

1970: Dave closes PDI and joins BDM.

1979: Dave resigns from BDM and joins Booz Allen Hamilton.

Early 1980s: First high-tech entrepreneurs begin companies in New Mexico; the New Mexico Entrepreneurs Association organizes.

1983: Santa Fe Private Equity, New Mexico's first venture capital firm, opens.

1985: Dave returns to Albuquerque, becomes Western Region Managing Partner of Booz Allen. New Mexico Business Innovation Center, Albuquerque's first business incubator, opens.

1986: Federal Technology Transfer Act passes. Dave becomes a senior partner and member of the Booz Allen's Operating Council.

1987: Legislature starts new program: State Investment Council can invest in venture capital funds.

April 1988: Dave acquires New Business Associates (NBA).

November 1988: Dave and partners found Quatro Corp.

January 1989: Quatro begins operations. NBA becomes a subsidiary.

1989: National Competitiveness Technology Transfer Act passes. Quatro learns about resonant ultrasound spectroscopy (RUS) at Los Alamos National Laboratory.

1990: Dave retires from Booz Allen Hamilton and joins Quatro. Honeywell Defense Avionics Systems contracts with Quatro for wire products manufacturing. Quatro creates Cable Technologies Corp. (CTC). Dave joins Sen. Jeff Bingaman's Tech Transfer Advisory Committee and organizes TEAM New Mexico (Technology Exploitation Access Management).

1992: Quatro licenses resonant ultrasound spectroscopy from Los Alamos National Laboratory. Quatro develops environmentally conscious electronics manufacturing; forms Ecocircuits Inc., a subsidiary, to market the factory design. CTC wins U.S. Senate Productivity Award.

1992: Dave is chairman, Technical Advisory Group, New Mexico Manufacturing Productivity Center; member, Task Force on Financing and Business Start-ups; member, New Mexico Quality Council's private sector working group (resulted in the formation of Quality New Mexico); president, Electrical and Computer Engineering Academy, NMSU and advisor to Dean of College of Engineering, NMSU; member, Task Force on Manufacturing for the Joint Economic Development Initiative.

1993: Quatro creates new division, Quatrosonics, around resonant ultrasound spectroscopy. NBA becomes Quatro Technologies.

1993: Dave joins Governor's Technical Excellence Committee (GTEC), becomes first chairman of Industry Network Corp. (INC), joins Riotech board, and starts a business newsletter, New Mexico Business Watch. Martin Marietta (later Lockheed Martin) creates Technology Ventures Corporation.

1994: Quatro Technologies identifies two promising ventures: Muse and HealthFirst. Quatrosonics becomes subsidiary of Quatro.

1994: TVC holds first New Mexico Equity Capital Symposium, Dave becomes symposium advisor. UNM creates Science & Technology Corporation. Sandia begins Technology Transfer Leave of Absence program. Coronado Ventures Forum begins. State Investment Council makes its first venture investment in ARCH Venture Partners.

1995: MuSE Technologies Inc. is founded.

1996: Quatro reorganizes. Two business units separate. Dave retains Quatro Manufacturing and Quatro Technologies. Quatro Manufacturing becomes Quatro Products Group. Quatro Technologies becomes Quatro Ventures.

1998: MuSE Technologies goes public.

1999: Quatro Ventures sells MuSE stock for a substantial gain. Dave and Quatro Ventures invest in Innovasic; Dave leads first venture round. Randy Burge organizes New Mexico Information Technology and Software Association. George Richmond organizes angel investor group, New Mexico Private Investors.

2000: Tech bubble bursts.

2000: Quatro Products Group wins contract with Honeywell's Home and Building Controls Division. Dave spins out Quatro Ventures and Quatro Products Group as separate companies owned by Dave and Quatro shareholders. Quatro Products becomes Quatro Systems Inc. Quatro Corporation ceases operations. Valley Ventures II invests in Quasar (formerly Quatrosonics); Dave becomes Quasar board member. Quatro Ventures invests in Introbotics and Elisar Software. Dave invests in Digital Traffic Systems (DTS). HealthFirst is acquired; Quatro Ventures realizes a gain. Legislature creates New Mexico Small Business Investment Corp. with funds from the Severance Tax Permanent Fund.

Late 2000: Quatro Systems sues Honeywell Home and Building Controls Division for failure to meet contract obligations. Quatro Systems files Chapter 11 bankruptcy petition.

2002: Quatro Systems and Honeywell settle. Dave liquidates Quatro Systems. Dave and Lem Hunter create Hunter Products; Dave and Quatro

Ventures invest. Hunter Products merges with Mechtronic Solutions Inc. (MSI). Valley Ventures III invites Dave to be special limited partner. Quatro Ventures invests in Elisar's second venture round. Dave invests in Exagen.

2003: Dave, Ray Radosevich and Tom Stephenson found Verge Fund. Elisar Software goes out of business.

2004: Verge and Dave invest in ZTEC. Dave and Quatro Ventures invest in Samba Holdings. The New Mexico Venture Capital Association is founded.

2005: Verge invests in PatchWork Systems, Altela, and TruTouch Technologies.

2006: Verge leads second round investment in Altela and first and second round in Wellkeeper; Verge invests in Quadric and BoomTime. Verge named a Top 100 Venture Capital Firms for Entrepreneurs by Entrepreneur Magazine.

2007: DTS acquired. MSI spins out Vibrant Corp.; Dave invests. Verge leads first round investments in Altaview Technologies, Vertical Power, Nuvita, and Avasca. Verge also invests in IntelliCyt and Noribachi. Verge establishes headquarters and incubator in former J.S. Brown Mercantile Building. Altaview, Altela, BoomTime, Quadric and Vertical Power locate in the new building.

2008: Dave turns 70. Verge creates Line of Equity to finance early stage companies and invests in Vibrant's second seed round.

Appendix I

How to Write a Business Plan

If you're writing a business plan to persuade investors, it helps to think like an investor.

"There are two sides of a business plan: What do I as an entrepreneur think that means? And what does the investor understand? The entrepreneur writes a business plan from his or her own perspective, trying to understand what an investor wants," Dave said. "There's usually a disproportionate share on the technology and product. Instead of pages and pages on 'This is my widget and here's how it works,' there should be one page. There should be more on who cares and how much money can I make with it.

"Most entrepreneurs have no business or financial perspective going in. That's not what makes them tick. They're frequently motivated by solving some problem. The investor's goal is to figure out how to make money."

The plan should show that you have a product, understand the customer, know how to reach the customer, have a realistic projection of sales and know how to build a team.

"Every time I go through a business plan, I look at how they project sales," Dave said. "They're not doing themselves any favors by over-committing. If you say you'll do X and you don't, you look stupid. I say, let's do something realistic and achievable. The business plan is the vehicle you use to convince me you're got it figured out."

Said Ron McPhee: "Your people are your business, so you need to spend a good chunk of thought describing your team and why this is the right team to accomplish the objective. When you do that, you may realize you don't have the right team. That's when the board can shore up those inadequacies."

The advice to entrepreneurs is typically to write the plan first and the executive summary last.

"Everybody wants to do the executive summary last," Dave said. "I say, write it first. It's an agonizing process, but it forces you to deal with strategic issues before you get lost in details. I've seen a lot of business plans, and often the entrepreneur doesn't have a sensible product roadmap or business model. By writing the executive summary first you see quickly what your business is. Or isn't."

Writing the executive summary first is not only good mental exercise, it keeps the entire plan concise and to the point. Business plans shouldn't weigh as much as War and Peace.

"I wrote business plans in briefing format and still prefer to have a plan in this format," said Dave. "I've found that the more words it takes for somebody to describe to you what their business is, the less they know about what they're doing. I'm also really big on graphics. I like to show the interactions of what you're trying to do. Visualization and graphics are huge for me. Do your flow charts before trying to put words down. Critical Path Analysis is also important. Understand how you're going to do things and what things really matter."

Business plans have an order and format:

1. Cover sheet. This should include the business name, date, address, telephone number, email address and Web site. A surprising number of business plans fail to include contact information.

2. Executive summary. Describe the business, state your goals, and summarize the business plan. Briefly describe your products or services, your marketing strategy, your management team and your financial projections. The executive summary will sell your proposal. It should be clear and concise, no longer than three pages. It should stand on its own and tell a compelling story about what this product will do and what problem it will solve.

3. Table of contents.

4. History. Relate how the company began, who the founders are, and how the product or services have evolved.

5. Business. What is your business? What do you do? Explain clearly. Avoid buzzwords. Investors are tired of hearing about paradigms shifting and technology disruption. What's really different about what you do?

6. Market. This is one of the most important sections of the business plan. Identify and define the markets. Who will buy? How do they buy? Do you have marketing professionals on board? Who is the competition? How big is the market?

7. Product or service. Describe your current products and services and any new products under development. Describe your research and development and intellectual property (patents, trademarks or copyrights). The product description should be in non-technical language. (Don't assume venture capitalists are software engineers.)

8. Management team. Provide the relevant background of key players and describe the organizational structure. Who is responsible for what? The experience of management team members should be relevant to their positions and to the business.

9. Finance. Describe pricing and project revenues and profits, sales program. Include current financial statements. The business plan should logically and clearly lead into the financial plan. Frequently it doesn't.

Appendix II

Quatro Technology Venture Evaluation Criteria

Evaluating the business potential of early-stage, high-tech companies is both complex and somewhat subjective. Determining the value of the newest companies—those with products still in or barely out of the laboratory—is particularly difficult.

After evaluating hundreds of opportunities, Dave and his colleagues at Quatro developed checklists to assure that all the right questions got asked. These checklists continue to evolve to serve each user's specific needs. They're intended to be used by experienced investors, but can be used by entrepreneurs, given a little training.

You must consider a number of technical, commercial and financial factors.

The technical evaluation determines the product's uniqueness, technical readiness and stage of development. This helps an investor understand the product's potential market impact and the cost and effort it will take to get it to market. Many high-tech product ideas are rejected at this point because the technical concept isn't really proven, there isn't enough demand for it, the intellectual property is weak, or it just isn't a market of interest to a specific investor.

The commercial evaluation digs deeper into the market potential for the product, the competition, the company's readiness to commercialize the product, and the time and money it will take to get the product to market. Most technically trained entrepreneurs have no appreciation for the complexity and importance of a well thought out commercialization plan. This process helps the investor understand the company's readiness to commercialize a product, AND it's very educational for the entrepreneur.

The financial evaluation determines if the payoff potential for the company is worth the investment. If the product passes the technical and commercial assessments, the next questions are: What's the risk? And what's the financial return? As it is with the commercial evaluation, most entrepreneurs need a lot of help with the financial evaluation. The financial checklist, like the others, is only a screening tool, and the financial estimates at this point are usually based on cursory market analysis or the investor's experience and judgment. Again, the purpose of this evaluation is to understand each opportunity well enough to eliminate those that don't fit the investor's strategy and to establish priorities for those that make the cut.

Most investors pursue less than 5 percent of the opportunities presented to them by entrepreneurs. These technology-venture-evaluation criteria are useful as a screening tool for investors and as a training tool for entrepreneurs. This process frequently reveals holes in the entrepreneurs' planning or thinking and helps them focus on the important issues. This evaluation process also helps the investor eliminate deals that don't fit their criteria with the minimum use of his time.

Here are examples of the checklists:

New Venture Criteria–Technical		
Technical Success Factors	*Score*	*Comments*
1) Potential Application & Products		
1 Market segment and/or application	2	
2 Market segments and/or applications	5	
Greater than 2 Market segments and/or applications	10	
2) Technical Innovation		
Some improvement over existing technology	1	
Incremental improvement over existing technology	4	
Breakthrough/Next Generation Technology	10	
3) Technology Development Plans/Requirements		
No existing written development plan	0	
Developmental plan conceived	2	
Written developmental plan	5	
Complete, structured developmental plans/requirements	10	
4) Manufacturing Capability		
No support facilities available	0	
Laboratory facilities Operational	2	
Developmental facility available	6	
Manufacturing Facilities Available	10	
5) State-of-the-Technology		
Concept only, no demonstration	0	
Technology in the form of breadboard	2	
Technology in the form of benchscale	4	
Technology in the form of a prototype	8	
Technology Fully Documented, Manuf. Resources Avail.	10	
6) Status of Intellectual Property		
Concept only, published papers of R&D	0	
Documented Lab books & research materials on file	4	
Copyrights on related publications	5	
Patent Filed	8	
Patent	10	
7) Access to Technical Talent/Support		
Inventor not available	0	
Inventor/P.I. available 25%	3	
Inventor/P.I. available 50%	6	
Inventor/P.I. available as required/or not required	10	
TOTAL	/ 70	

New Venture Criteria–Commercial		
Commercial Success Factors	*Score*	*Comments*
1) Potential Market Size, Potential & Growth		
Single niche and or fad appeal	2	
Mkt limited to one (1) segment such as defense only	5	
Multiple mkt sectors such as telecomm. & information systems	10	
2) Market Entry, Access & Distribution		
Mkt is understood, mkt entry will be based on own exp. curve	1	
Some existing distr & support networks, some work force devel	6	
Rapid introduction & reception to the market in less than 2 years with known dist. network	10	
3) Competition		
Highly skilled mkting and technical staffs with loyal customers	0	
Close knit user community with limited access	2	
Aging, entrenched ind With limited R&D budg. & prof. margins	5	
No dominant competitors with >15% of market, fragmented, no related customer loyalty	10	
4) Risks–Social/Political, Regulatory/Certification		
Product/application may be subject to imposition of tariffs, regulatory control, etc.	0	
Neutral to these areas	5	
Provides incentives for use, meets strong social pressures and desires/needs	10	
5) Strategic Alliances & Partnering		
Strategic alliances & partnering are unknown	0	
Strategic alliances targeted to applications are identified	3	
Strategic discussions and demos are planned/completed	5	
Strategic alliance/partnership is established	10	
6) Management Team		
Technical manager with agile team support	2	
Basic oper.mgmt.team established, selective augmentation plans	5	
Team fully assembled, known to business, finance & tech.comm	10	
7) Cost/Performance Advantage		
Cost & performance data is not known	0	
Cost & performance are equal to the competition	2	
Provides customers with 2 - 4 times performance adv at comparable cost	6	
Provides customers with a 5 - 10 times perf adv at comp cost	10	
8) Potential Customer Interest		
No customer interest perceived	0	
Customer desires some descriptive data	2	
Customer requests a site visit and technical data	4	
Customer voices a need and requests pricing & delivery data	8	
Interest in the product, supportive and may provide support (testing, funding, etc.)	10	
9) Time to Market		
Design is conceptual, no plan developed, qualif req in question	2	
Design can be complete in 12 - 18 months	4	
Design can be complete in 6 months	5	
Prototype can be tested within 12 months	8	
Product can reach the market within 18 months	10	
TOTAL	/ 90	

194

New Venture Criteria–Financial		
Financial Success Factors	*Score*	*Comments*
1) Return on Investment (ROI)		
<15% per year	1	
15 to 25% per year	5	
25 - 50% per year	8	
>50% per year	10	
2) Expected Sales and Revenues		
Breakeven at 4 - 5 years of operations	1	
Breakeven at 2 - 3 years of operations	2	
Breakeven at 2 years of operations	6	
Breakeven at 1 year of operations	10	
3) Potential Profit Margins (net)		
1 - 4% per year	1	
3 - 6% per year	4	
5 - 10% per year	6	
>10% per year	10	
4) Interest in Funding Sources		
Funding needs identified, sources unknown	1	
Business plan being developed, funding requirements known	2	
Business plan complete, funding sources targeted, plans submitted, favorable reception	5	
Funding sources available, comments in hand	8	
Funding sources available, comments agreed to, cash in hand	10	
5) Financial Risks		
Funding is available for six months based on part time staffing	0	
Cost, schedule are under development with one year operations window	1	
Business Plan has been funded for start-up requirements	5	
Business Plan has been funded and contingencies have been addressed	10	
6) Potential Sales or Revenues		
<$10M per year	1	
$10M - $100M per year	4	
$100M - $500M per year	8	
>$500M per year	10	
TOTAL	/ 60	

Index

Printed in the United States
122846LV00001B/59/P